Back on the Menu

I spend a lot of time training and developing my team.

Back on the Menu

My rollercoaster life

Conrad Gallagher

A. & A. Farmar

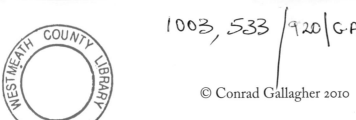
British Library Cataloguing in Publication Data
A CIP catalogue record for this book is available
from the British Library

ISBN: 978-1-906353-25-4

This edition first published in 2010 by
A. & A. Farmar Ltd
78 Ranelagh Village, Dublin 6, Ireland
Tel +353-1-496 3625 Fax +353-1-497 0107
Email afarmar@iol.ie
Web www.aafarmar.ie

Picture credits
Frontispiece, 65, 67, 70, 79, 89 Brian Daly
9, 39 Gallagher family
24 Great Northern Hotel
32, 34, Renvyle House Hotel
49 Waldorf Astoria Hotel
57 Hotel de Paris
68 Walter Pfeiffer
107 Jim Henderson
142 Maxwell

Printed and bound by ColourBooks
Designed by A. & A. Farmar
Typeset and indexed by Bookworks
Cover design by Kevin Gurry

Contents

To
Mum and Dad
who have never let me down

To
my darling wife, Candice
whose strength and perseverance
motivate me every day, and

To
my most special treasures
Lauren, Chandler and Conor

Prologue

SOMETHING DIDN'T FEEL RIGHT. Five bulky guys in dark blue bomber jackets were striding towards us. Across the street two black trucks with flashing lights were parked half on the kerb, half on the road. Then two more guys came from the other side. I looked at my doorman, but he had his hands full with the crazy queue—everyone dressed up to the nines, jostling, flirting, laughing, people we didn't want trying to get in . . . the usual . . .

I looked back—all seven guys blatantly jumped the queue.

'Are you Conrad Gallagher?' said one of them in my face.

'Who wants to know?'

'We're from the US Marshals service. You're under arrest.'

Then they dropped me to the ground with a knee in the back of my leg and rammed another into my spine. I felt my arms twisted behind my back, handcuffs slicing my wrists and hands going at my pockets and legs as if I had a bomb, and all the time questions and orders firing at me:

'Are you carrying any weapons? Lay down, stay down. Do not move, sir. Sir, do not move.'

Then they shouted my rights. I'd seen it a thousand times on TV but here it was being barked at me on the New York streets outside my own bar:

'You have the right to remain silent. Anything you say can and will be used against you in a court of law. You have the right to speak to an attorney . . .'

I screamed at my doorman to call my brother and they dragged me up off the ground and threw me into the van.

I sat shell-shocked, my hands cuffed behind my back, staring through the grille at the road opening up in front of me. What was going on? I wasn't an IRA guy on the run, I wasn't a Colombian drug baron—I was just a chef from Donegal . . .

Chapter 1
Mad to learn

MY LIFE IS NOT NORMAL. I don't get home at 6 o'clock and have time to put my feet up and watch TV or go to the gym. Five evenings a week I'm in one or other of my restaurants, sometimes both, cooking, training staff, talking to customers and managing crises. Most nights I get home after 11—that's hard on my family. Where does the drive to do this come from? Not just once, or for a few years, but for twenty years?

The simple answer is food is my passion. Every day my head is buzzing with ideas about new dishes and new combinations. When I go into the restaurant kitchens all the day-to-day problems go out the window. I absolutely love it—there are so many techniques and skills involved in cooking and it's total concentration.

I was lucky—I discovered it was my vocation early on in life. My greatest pleasure as a child was to bake with my mother and my granny. From the earliest of ages I'd be out licking the bowl before it was washed, sprinkling flour over the counter, decorating little buns or adding the chocolate to Rice Krispie cakes. We always had good food, not gourmet, but there was an effort put into it and the house was always full of the sounds of cooking, whether bacon sizzling on the pan in the early morning, onions being chopped or stock simmering on the stove at all hours.

I remember my mother's version of Irish stew—to me it meant comfort and the most loved feeling you could ever experience. I still think hers is the best you can find—lamb, carrots, leeks, onions, potatoes, stock, a couple of bay leaves and white pepper. When I was about eight I started making it myself but of course I didn't do it exactly the way my mother did, I'd add extra vegetables—carrots, leek, parsnips, celery—and finish it with heavy cream and chopped parsley. This made it colourful and creamy and I used to love the feeling I got when it came out really well.

Food was the great cure-all. 'Eat that up now,' my granny would say, 'that'll be good for you.' If you had a bad stomach you'd boil up some nettles from the fields and add a spoonful of vinegar and some sugar to make it taste better and then you'd strain it and drink it like tea. For a sore throat you'd drink hot lemon juice with honey and to keep the flu away you'd eat raw garlic.

And I was mad to learn everything I could. My father showed me how to do a mixed grill with liver and bacon, and I still remember his advice about chicken soup: 'You have to use proper stock made from bones to make good soup'. I'd get him to taste something I'd made and he'd say 'Oh, Conrad, that's really lovely.' Of course, he might have been putting me on! My mother showed me how to make black pudding—sheep's blood, sheep's stomach, porridge oats and onions—I'd watch her mix it all up and put it inside the stomach and then my granny sewing it up. They used to leave it to boil and boil all night long—until the dogs came barking at the back door attracted by the smell! But whatever I was learning, it came naturally to me and I enjoyed it.

The kitchen was home to me, whether I was baking bread or cooking apple pie, or doing the breakfast when my mother took in lodgers for B&B. And after a while I was in the kitchen so much, they were able to just tell me what to do and let me get on with it: 'Put ten slices of bacon under the grill, can you cut the tomatoes, and boil off some potatoes,' so it got to the stage that my mother was making the beds and I was cooking the breakfast.

Sometimes my dad said to me I should be out playing football like everybody else. He's a huge sports fan like all the family—anything to do with a ball whether it's golf, tennis, football or cricket, he's glued to it. But sport didn't appeal to me at all, either watching or playing. I had absolutely no interest in it. If it was on the television I'd walk out of the room. If it was on the radio I'd go outside. To look forward to going to a football match on a Saturday—that wasn't for me. There was only one place I wanted to be.

But I'd get very frustrated if something didn't turn out properly, if a carrot cake didn't rise enough, or the sausages weren't brown enough—it would really upset me. (My little son is the same—he'll spend a whole day perfecting muffins.) It is this constant striving for perfection that distinguishes the great from the ordinary run of the mill. And I think some of these driven people have obsessive compulsive disorder. I swear a lot of chefs are borderline OCD—they are never satisfied, they concentrate intensely—you can see it etched on their face—and they think about it all the time. If you don't have that obsessive, perfectionist streak, you'll never be a top chef.

BACK ON THE MENU

My family

I was born in a little Donegal town off the north-west coast of Ireland called Ballyshannon in March 1971. It has a population of 2,000 and claims to be the oldest town in Ireland. Rory Gallagher, the great Irish guitarist, was born there as well. When I was about two years old my parents moved about twenty miles north-east to Letterkenny, my mother's home town, to a regular little housing estate called Hawthorn Heights, not far from Derry City. They still live there to this day. Letterkenny is the biggest town in Donegal; about 18,000 people live there now but it was much smaller back then.

At first, there was just Keith, my older brother, and myself; the younger two—Claudine and Vernon—came along much later. I was christened Finian, with Conrad as my second name, but I was always known as Conrad. My parents called us unusual names because there are so many Gallaghers in Donegal. If you have a traditional first name you'll be given another one—like the TD Pat 'The Cope' Gallagher, and my friends Paddy 'The Gate' and Jimmy 'The Lodge'.

As young kids we often went to my great aunt's farm in Glenswilly, just outside Letterkenny. We'd milk the cows and round up the sheep. One day when I was very small, maybe three or four, we were being minded there while my parents went to a wedding. I wandered off and no one could find me. Search parties went out looking for me and my parents were called back but there was no sign of me.

Next morning my grandfather found me, safe

and sound under a fairy tree. (Fairy trees are all over Donegal—hawthorns, ash or oaks and they're regarded as sacred so you'd never cut them down or damage them or you'd have bad luck—the fairies would get you.) It was so cold and wet my mother thought that angels had protected me from harm. She always says she went to Mass every morning for weeks afterwards. Some people wonder if I was traumatised by this but I have no memory of it at all.

My father, Michael, comes from a little place outside Donegal town called Laghey. His father was a garda, but also a part-time farmer—he had a lot of land. In those days all the land was left to the oldest brother so my father knew, being the second son, that when my grandfather died there would be nothing left for him. So he got a job as a technician with the telephone company P&T, which became Telecom Éireann and then Eircom.

My mother, Evelyn Monaghan, grew up with her four brothers in Letterkenny, in the Burmah council housing estate. People are very proud of being from there. To this day, people will come up to me and say 'I remember your mother from the Burmah.' Her father was a nurse in St Conal's mental hospital, which didn't pay too well of course. And going to college in those days meant a five-hour bus drive to Dublin, plus lodgings, books and fees.

There was no way you could do that on a nurse's salary, and anyway he died young, so my granny took in lodgers, just as my mother would do. All four boys did well—the eldest, Hugo is a paediatrician in Our Lady's Hospital for Sick Children in Crumlin; Frankie is a successful businessman in Letterkenny—I'm very close to him, we're like brothers; Eamon was doorman for years in Peacock Alley, we used to call him 'the jackhammer'; Terry, the youngest, went to Harvard and got a doctorate in psychiatry.

Schooldays

I hated schoolwork—it bored me to tears. I reckon I'm dyslexic which didn't help. It's still a problem—some days I could write a letter to the Pope, on others I wouldn't be able to spell dog. In those days of course dyslexia wasn't properly recognised. There was still corporal punishment so all you'd get was a good caning. I remember once one of the Brothers caned me so hard my hand swelled up—I'd turned it so he hit me across the knuckles and broke one. My father came up to the school and challenged him. He's tall like me but he's a very civil, calm man. Growing up—we were never put down, never told 'just sit there and be quiet.' But he always defended his kids: if neighbours complained that we were out playing ball in the street he would say 'Were you never young yourselves?'

I also had a very bad stammer—I just couldn't get the words out. My parents sent me to Mrs Saddler for elocution lessons to see if I could be cured. She must have helped or else I grew out of it because I've no trouble now except when I'm tired or stressed.

I was one of hundreds of boys at the local national school, Scoil Colmcille on Convent Road, run by the Presentation Brothers. My red hair and freckles automatically gave me the name of 'Ginger'. Then after Columcille at the age of twelve I went to a Christian Brothers school called St Eunan's College.

Myself aged seven or eight

I've nothing good to say about the Brothers—they suppress people and I hated every minute I spent there. There was one decent teacher though, Mr Coyle, who taught woodwork. I liked him and I did well because I enjoyed carpentry—I did well at anything to do with using my hands. One thing I learned there was that if I could find a job where I could use my hands, there would be no more classrooms and no more Brothers hitting you with a cane and then trying to feel you up ten minutes later!

Not surprisingly, I started mitching. My two best friends were David Donnelly and Liam McCann and we all hated school. We spent many days up at Roger's Burn, sitting in the sun, swimming in the pond. In those days it was fields and fields, basically farmland, with horses and donkeys, a river and places to swim. As we got a bit older, the mischief began, we'd mitch from school and head up there and ride the horses and donkeys around the fields. I have very fond memories of that place. It's all housing estates now.

The Troubles were a big part of my life growing up in Donegal in the seventies and eighties. We'd always go into the North on Saturdays for our shopping—there was a bigger variety of things to buy and a lot cheaper—and Strabane was just ten miles away over the Border. We passed through the RUC checkpoints where the British Army guys would check my father's driving licence and tell him to open the boot, pointing cameras under the car to see if there was a bomb. Donegal was rampant with IRA and INLA at that time; naturally we knew all the names as we'd see them around. The Troubles left a big impression on me like everybody else, a lot of bitter memories.

To work

From an early age I was working hard and earning money. I was the anxious second child, wearing hand-me-downs, attuned to my parents' financial worries. I wasn't demanding and I liked to make a contribution. As well as everything I did in the house helping out with the lodgers, I always had regular jobs. My first job at the age of about seven was delivering bread with my mother's cousin, Hughie McDaid. We'd stack the shelves in the supermarkets and go door-to-door around Letterkenny and surrounding towns, selling bread, buns and cakes. I could eat as many cream buns as I liked and got paid for the pleasure. Hughie didn't drink or smoke and was apparently worth a fortune. Later, I had a paper round after school. I would pick up about a hundred evening papers and go round the houses selling them. I made about a penny a paper.

Then, when I was about eight, the local milkman,

Paddy Ferry, asked me to help him with his milk round. He was a chain smoker, he taught me to drive the van and every word that came out of his mouth was a curse word. I thought he was the coolest guy ever.

He would knock on my door at six in the morning—of course my mother and my granny were already up —'Are you up, Connier?'—and I'd be up and out, holding onto the back of the van, rain, sleet or snow, delivering bottles of milk to half of Letterkenny as they slept. Paddy had another helper, Jamie McBrearty, who was fifteen, and smoked twenty Major a day, or sometimes my friends Christy Culer or Mark Moore would help as well. We used to make as much noise as possible approaching our headmaster's house—loud animal noises. When he found out who was doing it, we got caned. I did the milk round until nine a.m. when I was dropped off at school. On Saturdays we stocked up the van for the next week. I collected my money on Friday night—£7 for the week— and gave £5 to my mother and kept £2 for myself; £2 bought a lot of sweets and single cigarettes from Róise's sweet shop in Main Street.

Paddy used to breed Jack Russell dogs—they have their tails docked soon after they're born. One Saturday I came across these day-old puppies whose tails Paddy had chopped off. I tried to be tough but I remember being dropped off at the house and never feeling as bad about anything. It was probably the first time in my life that I felt really, really sad.

Somewhere between the ages of ten and twelve I went from being four foot tall to over six foot—I ended up at six foot four. Being tall for my age meant I could pass for much older than I was, and I was able for hard physical work. Every winter for a good few years I went picking potatoes with some of my classmates for two or three weeks. It was backbreaking work but it was worth it for the few weeks as it was very well paid. I'd arrange with my parents, Paddy Ferry and the paper shop to be away for that time and I tried to make as much money as I could.

The day started in the freezing cold and pitch dark, ten or twelve of us standing at the end of the road, waiting for the truck to come and pick us up. With our flasks of tea and sandwiches, we would climb into the back of the truck which would drive for twenty or thirty minutes out into the countryside till we got to the farm. There we stood, teeth chattering, until we were each given a stand of potatoes. Then the digger came along the furrow turning up the potatoes, and we'd be off, shouting 'Come on the digger!' because the more potatoes we picked and ran over and dumped, the more we were paid.

We'd be given plastic basins and then we'd fall to our knees or down on all fours, whatever worked best, and pick away like mad because if you didn't work good and hard, fast and furious, you wouldn't get back the next day. By the end of the day, the muck would be literally hanging off you. There were all ages—I was always the youngest—from all walks of life, young lads like me, the unemployed and guys who would schedule their work holidays for that time to make extra money. I got paid £7 or £8 a day, which was massive compared to the £7 a week I got from Paddy the milkman. So by the end of it, I'd always have a huge chunk of money.

One year when my parents were going through a

bit of a lean time, a sheep ran out on the road and my father crashed his car into it, doing a huge amount of damage that was going to cost £108 to fix, which was a lot of money in those days. And we couldn't claim on the insurance because if you claimed it trebled the premium. So I gave my dad my potato money to fix the car. It was fine; I got great pleasure out of doing it and it made my father proud, I think. To this day, every time he has a couple of drinks he brings it up.

Chapter 2
My apprenticeship

THE MILK ROUND AND THE POTATO PICKING were just some of the casual jobs that I did over the years and they earned me good money. But the one that set me on the road to being a chef was in the kitchen of the Ballyraine Hotel in Letterkenny. One summer when I was ten or eleven and still at national school the hotel was short staffed. The Donegal International Rally was on—it's held every June and starts and finishes in Letterkenny and of course the town is packed during those days.

The hotel manager at the time, Pat McGarvey, was a friend of my father's. He was the most stylish man I had ever seen. He wore beautiful suits, shirts embroidered with his monogram, and silver cufflinks, and he always smelled strongly of after-shave. It was known around the neighbourhood that I had a huge interest in food, so Pat rang my father and said, 'We're under fierce pressure here. That young lad of yours knows how to cook—could you send him up to give us a hand over the weekend.' He probably didn't realise how young I was. My parents were doubtful about letting me go but I managed to persuade them. I told the hotel I was fifteen—I got away with it because I was so tall.

It was like a whole new world opening up to me. The hotel kitchen was huge. There were people running around everywhere—chefs, waiters, waitresses, dishwashers. One of the dishwashers was wearing a crash helmet. I found out that he was on day release from the mental hospital and when things got too much for him he would bang his head against the wall. I was warned not to touch his blue cloth. 'That's Paddy's—he gets very upset if anyone touches his cloth.'

But if Paddy was a bit manic he was nothing to Jimmy, the head chef. He had a really bad temper and everyone was afraid of him. When you heard him clip-clopping in his clogs you'd shiver in your boots. The waiting staff were afraid to speak. A waitress once dropped a plate and Jimmy exploded. Everybody ducked, then ran for cover. There were lids, saucepans, containers, and plates flying through the air. Eventually it all calmed down and everybody came back and went on as if nothing had happened.

That was my introduction to the mad world of hotel kitchens—and I loved it. I couldn't wait to go back. The first day they had me sweeping, breaking boxes and fetching and carrying—general kitchen porter stuff. The next day Pat brought me into one of the sculleries and said 'Meet Lucy.' Lucy was a big black dustbin that had to be filled each day with enough peeled potatoes to feed half of Donegal, be it a funeral, wedding or christening. So I spent the whole of that shift peeling potatoes.

Pat then gave me a uniform and a hat and brought me into the cold starter section. He showed me a plate with lettuce, tomatoes, cucumbers, hard-boiled eggs, a tub of mayonnaise and a jar of paprika and said 'A hundred and twenty eggs mayonnaise, please. And we need melon starters—slice them into halves, then quarters, then eighths.' The waiters would come in shouting their orders—'Two egg mayonnaise, two melon, give me four shrimp cocktail'. I was flying, I could do that. At the end of the shift, Pat paid me and asked me to come in and help with the breakfast in the morning. And of course, that was my forte. I could do breakfast. Mind you, doing it for hundreds was a lot different from doing it for ten or fifteen.

From the moment I started, I tried to learn as much as I could. I worked hard and got to know the chefs and so I was asked back after school, the weekends and in the holidays. Sometimes I worked as bar back, collecting and washing the glasses. I'd take orders for drinks and run around the nightclub at night.

But my parents weren't happy—I was mitching school, working all hours in the hotel—they'd find out that I hadn't been at school and they'd go crazy, call the hotel and say that I couldn't work, that I had to go to school. But I was a stubborn boy and two days later I would be back in the kitchen.

And I got on the right side of Jimmy—with a little help from the head waiter. 'Now, if you want to get on with Jimmy,' he said, 'come in early in the morning and turn the oven on, and get his chef's jacket from the office and fold it over a chair in front of the oven and make it nice and warm for him. And make him a nice cup of tea.'

I'd been there long enough to know that that would probably work.

'And he loves his sausage sandwich in the morning,

two slices of bread, butter, ketchup and a couple of sausages between them and cut that in half. So when he comes in tomorrow say "Good morning, Chef, there's your breakfast, there's your jacket" and just keep walking and he'll feel bad then giving out to you.' And it worked. They all got to rely on me, especially Jimmy, and I started spending as much time as I could in the hotel kitchen.

In the meantime, the Ballyraine was taken over by the McEniff family, who were from the seaside resort town of Bundoran and owned two hotels there, the Holyrood and the Great Northern. They renamed the Ballyraine the Mount Errigal, after the highest mountain in Donegal. Half of Northern Ireland used to come out for the summer and the weekends to get away from the Troubles and there were busloads of Scottish, English and Welsh as well.

The McEniffs put up with Jimmy's temper because he was so good at his job, and having to staff three hotels they needed him. It was hard to get any chefs at that time, never mind good ones, and in those days it was serious graft. There was no such thing as buying in—you made everything. You'd do a wedding for four or five hundred—just three or four of you in the kitchen; turkey and ham for the main course, poached salmon for starter—good wholesome Irish food. Between roasting the turkeys, making the stuffing, peeling the potatoes, making the gravy—all from scratch, no packets—you'd be on your feet all day, never stopping; then there was breakfast, room service and bar service.

Chefs work just as many hours today, but the work is a lot more refined—meat and poultry come ready butchered but in those days the turkeys would be delivered with the feathers still on, the beef would come as a whole hindquarter so you'd have to pluck the poultry and butcher the meat as well as everything else.

I remember one day we were making mashed potato for a wedding of 500 people. Pots and pots of potatoes had to be peeled and boiled, then put into a big mixing machine. There were two connections at the top of the machine, one for the mixer and the other for the meat grinder. If only the mixer was attached and not the grinder, the grinder connection would still go round and round while the mixing was going on. It was always very greasy, and from time to time a big blob of oil would come out of the connection. I mixed up the potatoes, added the butter, the milk, the cream and the salt and pepper, set the mixer going and went off to check on something. When I came back the potatoes were grey. The oil had dumped into it. 'Merciful Jesus' I said (or maybe something else a lot stronger) 'these people are sitting down in half an hour!'

We had to delay the lunch. Every single person in the kitchen had to stop what they were doing, run over and peel as many potatoes as they could. Then we had to get in some instant mashed potato—Smash—get it going in another pot, cook the other potatoes, and put them in with the Smash. The grey stuff became staff dinner for a week.

Planning my future

The more time I spent in hotel kitchens and the more school I missed, the more unhappy my father got. He could see no future in it for me. Being a chef wasn't yet an acceptable career—that only happened after CERT (the training organisation) was created—and according to my dad, chefs were a little too fond of drinking and smoking and were always hanging around pubs on a Monday and Tuesday—'Sure, they're all misfits', he'd say. And of course this was before celebrity chefs came on the scene in a big way. I think the first chef I saw on TV was Keith Floyd, and I would have been aware of Ballymaloe and Myrtle Allen. 1003, 533 | 920 | GAL

My mother on the other hand could see that there could be a future in it for me. She's very smart and very driven and she always had big ideas for me. She wanted me to see the world, so she encouraged me. But the way she saw it, being a chef was just a stepping stone to the bigger prize—becoming a hotel manager. 'You'll hardly be cooking over a stove till you're fifty—if you go into hotel management you can become a boss.' Back then there was a proper hierarchy. In those days, being manager of the hotel meant being in charge and if you didn't have a Leaving Cert or huge academic skills, becoming a chef was the back door to becoming manager. It's different now—even if there's a manager, the chef is top dog. My mother's plan for me was that I'd get a job as a chef in a big hotel in France or Switzerland and then come back to Dromoland Castle or Ashford Castle—one of those places that she'd read about where Charlie Haughey and President Reagan stayed.

After some discussion then, my parents agreed that I could leave school after Group Cert, under the condition that I would go to Killybegs Catering College when I was fifteen.

BACK ON THE MENU

My first mentor

Once I'd left school, I was free to work at the Mount Errigal, which meant spending all my days with Jimmy, who might have been terrifying to some, but he took me under his wing. And because I was Jimmy's boy, nobody could mess me around.

Even at that age, every night after work I was out drinking and smoking and playing cards, but no matter what, every morning at 6 a.m. I'd get up and get to the kitchen. And, like the head waiter had told me, I would turn on the oven, pull up a chair and fold Jimmy's jacket over the back of the chair to warm it for him before he came in. Then I'd make him his tea and toast so the bear would have a full belly before he started.

Jimmy had a huge influence on me—he taught me about kitchens, respect for cooking, your chef and your teacher. We became so close, we developed almost a father/son type of relationship—mind you, that didn't stop him yelling at me. One day he blindfolded me to show me that cooking was as much about sounds as vision. 'If you can close your eyes and fry an egg you'll end up getting a natural feeling for food,' he said. He got me to listen to the pan heating up, the butter melting and the gentle sizzle when the egg hit the pan. Frying an egg is still the best way of testing whether someone can cook. Jimmy taught me so much that by the age of fourteen I was cooking on my own on his days off.

By then I was over six foot tall, had a mouth like a sewer and if anyone turned a word in my mouth in that kitchen there would be trouble.

CONRAD GALLAGHER

It *was* possible to lead a regular life if you were a chef. I saw this at the Holyrood Hotel when I was working there one summer. The head chef was Jim Herity—a lovely, calm, naturally teaching chef. He was married to the hotel receptionist, Mary. They had kids and he would pick them up from school. So I thought if Jim's got a wife and family and a house and a car then some sort of normality was possible.

Chapter 3
One of the boys

AT CHRISTMAS I WAS ASKED to work in the Great Northern in Bundoran. It was a much bigger hotel than the Mount Errigal and would mean living away from home. I was up for the challenge—I'd been working in a few cafés around town as well but really I was getting bored. And even though I'd have to leave home, my parents let me go because a lot of the teachers from the catering college worked there part time.

I wished my family a happy Christmas, and thumbed a lift across the Barnesmore Gap through the dark and wet. The staff quarters were outside the hotel; they were nicknamed 'H-Block' after the prison. We slept six or more to a room—it was cold and damp, and noisy, too, with the Atlantic Ocean roaring against the gable of the house.

At six o'clock on my first morning we were woken by a knock from the hotel's porter to get us up and to go to the kitchen. Somebody shouted 'Four hundred for breakfast!'. This time there were two Lucys. I had to spend three days peeling potatoes—with extra care because the potato peelings were checked to make sure not too much was wasted. So it was in at the deep end. I got a nose bleed early on—stress, I suppose, but I tried to hide it. The first night I went up to the staff quarters cramp set in.

Between the tiles they had on the floors and the cold in the kitchen and standing for hours the backs of my legs kind of locked. I remember crying with the pain. (That was where growing so fast in such a short time used to get me—in the backs of my legs. After work in the Mount Errigal my granny would rub poteen into the calves of my legs. She firmly believed that you never drank poteen, you rubbed it into your skin.)

The head waiter in the Great Northern, Albert Johnston, was always slagging me off. He was big and jolly, wonderful fun and always the life and soul of the party—we're still great friends today. He loved to tell the stories of Billy, the head chef, throwing cleavers at the managers and going over the counters after the waitresses and how he used to keep his motorbike in the kitchen and when the hygiene inspector visited he said it was the cleanest thing in the kitchen!

After the potatoes I was put on to fresh fruit salad—there were bins and bins of it. Then it was another section and then another and before I knew it I was getting closer to the big chefs at the hot stoves. During service one day a chef ran out of Hollandaise sauce and was too busy serving to stop. Like other classic French sauces it's based on Béarnaise sauce. So the head chef shouted, 'Can anybody make Béarnaise sauce?' I jumped at the chance and shouted 'Yes, Chef. Me, Chef.' About six minutes later I presented him with a beautiful, perfectly seasoned Béarnaise sauce. He smiled and sent me back to Lucy.

I had hardly started peeling again when he called me over and asked me had I ever cooked steak before. I replied 'Yes, Chef,' and he left me to watch the grill. I thought to myself 'That's it—I'm in! No more Lucys, no more peeling and chopping, I'm in the main kitchen now.' When the service ended, and we'd cleaned down, the head chef asked me to come and see him. I stood there waiting but all he said was would I mind doing another bag of potatoes before knocking off? I was gutted. Later that night in H-Block we all laughed at how I'd been expecting praise—or a promotion.

Next morning, while I was filling Lucy, an argument broke out between the pastry chef and the head chef. Tempers flew and the pastry chef threw down his apron and walked out. This wouldn't usually be a huge problem, but it was six days before Christmas, the busiest time of year when a hotel takes in 30 per cent of its annual profits, and they had no pastry chef.

I already knew how to make all the classic desserts— Black Forest gâteaux, sherry trifle, baked Alaska, fresh

The Great Northern Hotel, Bundoran, Co. Donegal,
where aged fourteen I found out what being able to cook
got you—respect, money and girls.

fruit salad, apple tart, lemon meringue pie—as I'd been helping to make them for years. 'Chef,' I said, ' I can do pastry. Give me your recipe book and I'll work all day and all night and pastry won't be a problem.' He looked at me as if to say 'Who is this guy?' and then he said 'What can you make?'

'If you give me the recipes I can make all the desserts—just as good as the other guy.'

There were about 350 people booked for dinner. He decided to give me the chance, but he cut the number of desserts on the menu to four instead of seven. Then the butterflies in the stomach started—I was really nervous. But it turned out Chef didn't eat desserts and he didn't want to taste any of them. I had made sure the presentation was good so he was happy. From then on, I did all the desserts.

By the end of the Christmas season I knew everybody in the hotel by their first name and they knew me. I had landed, I wore a chef's hat and the waitresses made me tea and brought me drinks. They had all heard about the young guy on the desserts.

'Can you believe it,' they would say, 'Can you believe he's only fourteen?'

'No way! Only fourteen, he couldn't be—God he's only a baby.'

I knew then what being able to cook got you—respect, money and girls! And I knew that if I worked hard I could be great at the job.

The first time I saw really good food was when a French chef with a big moustache called Michel came to Bundoran for the summer season. He wasn't into turkey and ham. He would go down to Rossnowlagh Harbour for mussels and steam them with white wine and garlic. Instead of stew, he would bake lamb cutlets with aubergines, tomatoes, olives and courgettes in a big tin. He started doing steak au poivre, steak Diane, lobster Thermidor, sole meunière and sole Colbert—all the classic French dishes, all done properly. He transformed the dining room into a really nice place to come and eat. The prices went up and the head waiter no longer went around in a waistcoat and shirt and tie, he now had a tuxedo.

I worked with Michel for a whole season and learned a lot from him. He was a wild man for the drink and a wild man for the women. As soon as we finished work we'd go out together. Although I was only fifteen I was so tall I could pass for eighteen so I had no problem getting served in bars. Because Michel was French, and probably the only Frenchman in the town, the girls would go mad for him. I remember sitting up at the bar and watching him in action. He had barely any English but he was some goer! There were thousands of caravans in Bundoran, and he'd hook up with somebody and they'd disappear off. Then next morning I'd be in the hotel doing the breakfast and he'd call.

'Is the manager in yet? Does he know I'm not in? I'll be there later—I was in the caravans last night.'

I'd be covering for him the whole time. He was an awful playboy. And he used to be fond of his couple of pints in the afternoon and I'd be dragged away then as well.

All the time I'd been working in the various McEniff

hotels I'd been getting close to the family, Seán and Brian, and especially their mother, Mrs McEniff. It got to the stage where I had my own room in the hotel in Bundoran—I wasn't in the staff quarters any more, and there was more to my relationship with the McEniffs than just an employee. I was a good kid, I worked all day and all night and never complained, and I tried to do every task better each time. When they needed me, I'd be there thumbing lifts up and down, up and down between Bundoran and Letterkenny.

One morning, after I'd done the breakfast service, Mrs McEniff called me to go upstairs because a man had fainted in the corridor outside room 34. When I got there the doctor had arrived as well and he asked me to help move him back into the room. Then he said to me 'Do you realise he's dead?' He'd had a heart attack. He was the first dead man I'd ever seen and he'd just eaten my scrambled eggs! I was scared it was my fault he'd died so I was really relieved when I found out it wasn't my cooking that killed him. I went to Mass every day that week to give thanks.

Mrs McEniff was in her seventies. She baked all the bread for the hotels and was always the first in and the last to leave. If you were late you met with her sharp tongue, but she took a shine to me. I got to know the recipe for her bread—she never let anybody else see it. We'd chat away and she'd wake me for Mass on Sundays. I used to help her go round the bins at the end of the night to see if the chef had wasted any food. Then we'd separate the food for the pig man and while she washed her hands in the kitchen sink I'd go to the hotel laundry to get her clean towels. When she got her hair done on a Saturday I would whistle and say to her 'God, you look great today, Missus' and she would smile back at me.

I played a joke on her one very quiet Saturday, one of the very few that we didn't have a wedding. I walked out to reception, then came back in and told her the wedding guests had started to arrive. She jumped up and said 'What wedding?' Everybody else stood back and watched and waited for the explosion. Then I laughed, she laughed, and they realised it was a joke.

Catering college

By now, I was one of the boys. I was having a few pints, snogging the waitresses, watching all the shenanigans going on in the hotel and learning about life. I don't know whether they were good lessons or bad lessons—but I guess it was all part of growing up. So it was very difficult for me then to go back into school after the summer to catering college.

But a deal was a deal and I had to go. The McEniffs put in a good word for me with the school in Killybegs and I was accepted for a place. I was still only fifteen— too young, really, as you were supposed to be at least seventeen, and most of the students had their Leaving Certs. But because I had so much experience, and the McEniffs spoke well of me, I was accepted. The teachers at the college all had high regard for the McEniffs and wanted to work in their hotels on their time off, so they were willing to bend the rules for me.

Killybegs is a fishing port—I remember it as being cold and wet and the smell of fish was rampant, and it never seemed to stop raining, just like Bundoran. My fondest memories are of the guys I shared a room with in digs— Enda McCauley, Pat Fahey, John Luka from Cavan and Eugene Diver from Gweedore. One morning we woke up at 2 a.m. and moved the clocks forward to 6.30 a.m., woke everyone and told them we were late for class. We hid in the bathroom while the others ran off to class in the cold and wet. We went back to bed while the others stood around wondering why the school wasn't open. We were heroes as the story went around the school. Fran was another great character. He was only in the business for the waitresses and hostesses—the cooking was secondary. He thought it was the best job in the world.

Pat O'Callaghan was school principal and there were nearly as many stories about him as about Billy—how he locked students in the fridge, made a student eat 64 portions of quiche just because he picked off a corner to taste, hung girls by their bra straps from a meat hook because 'girls shouldn't be in a commercial kitchen'—all nonsense, of course.

Class started at 8 a.m., went on till 5 p.m., and then it was study from 7 p.m. to 9 p.m., and we were supposed to be in bed by 10.30 p.m. That was a big change for me and I found the discipline very hard.

On the first day we had to make wheaten bread, one loaf at a time. I'd been making all types of bread for years—wheaten bread, treacle bread, soda bread and fruit scones. When the teacher gave out the recipe I could immediately see a problem. The proportions were 100g white flour, 100g brown flour, a pinch of salt, a pinch of sugar, 25g of butter, 1 egg—and 1 pint of buttermilk.

So I said 'Sorry, teacher, this recipe won't work—it's too wet.' He looked at me and more or less told me to keep quiet. So I thought to myself, you can argue all you want but I'm doing it my way. I used a cup rather than a pint of buttermilk, moulded my bread into a nice shape, put a cross on top of it and popped it into the oven. Sure enough, when we opened the oven there were twenty-one pancakes and one perfect loaf of bread. It turned out that it was the teacher's first day too—we ended up good friends and still slag each other off.

In the next class, we had to bone a chicken. I had the chicken boned, my knife, bowl and chopping board cleaned, and the bones trimmed up on the tray ready for the stockpot by the time the others had the plastic off the wrapper. Of course, I'd been working in commercial kitchens for years whereas some of the other students didn't know their way round kitchens at all. I very quickly realised that there's a big gap between what happens in school and what happens in restaurants and hotels.

In school our days were taken up with learning the classic techniques and recipes, so I learned a lot and it has always stood to me. I really liked the teachers, I liked what they were doing. Mind you, some of the recipes we learned we'd never use in a commercial kitchen—things like béchamel sauce.

In class you do everything by the book, it's like being in a cocoon, but if you're in a hotel kitchen and there are a hundred people sitting waiting for lunch you can't operate as if you're in an ideal world. Students were sent out on work experience to various hotels and you could see how they changed after their first placement. They went out as students but they came back as workers. They learned that things move fast during service—you do what you have to do as quickly and as neatly as you can. And you try to keep Chef happy. 'Where are those pots?' 'Coming Chef!' even though you haven't even started washing them. 'Is that sauce ready?' 'Yes, Chef!' even though it needs to be reduced further. You don't question, you don't argue—all the elements must come together with split second timing so there's no room for hesitation or confrontation.

One weekend a month you could go home but I had a pass—I got out every weekend to go to work in the Great Northern. Every Friday, while everybody else talked about going to the Forest Hill disco on the Saturday, I would be thumbing up that dark road from Killybegs to Donegal town and on to Bundoran. I always had to work—they were depending on me at the hotel and anyway I needed the money. The grant wouldn't even have kept me in cigarettes. I'd get there by seven and I'd be straight into the kitchen in time to help with dinner. On Saturday I'd be going like mad for the wedding, then again for lunch on Sunday and then setting up for the early part of the week. Then I'd thumb back to Killybegs again on Sunday.

I was working very hard and I enjoyed it. I may have been the youngest at Killybegs, but I was the most experienced. The first year I was voted Best Student and that gave me a big boost. There were also benefits from being good at what I did. I had lots of friends, there was interest from girls . . .

And it led to one of the greatest breaks of my life, when Renvyle House Hotel in Connemara came calling. Hotels and restaurants used to look for good students to boost their staff over Christmas and other holiday periods. The Christmas of my second year, the manager at Renvyle called the college looking for someone to help out as pastry chef at Christmas and go back for Easter and the summer.

I heard later that the principal said, 'I've got one guy, Conrad Gallagher—he's very cocky, he'll listen to nobody, but he's very good at what he does.'

Everyone wanted to work at Renvyle House—it's one of the great country house hotels and we'd all heard about the head chef there, Tim O'Sullivan. He is a legend, very eccentric, bohemian and individual with long hair and an earring and one of the greatest Irish chefs. And he was about ten years ahead of his time. He served venison, sea bass, quail and pheasant—I'd never seen any of that

Renvyle House Hotel, Connemara, Co. Galway where I spent some of the happiest times of my life. I still go there whenever I can.

before—and he was doing escargots and frogs' legs when everyone else was doing fish with sauces. And each dish was complete in itself and properly balanced. There was no ordering the potatoes and vegetables separately, to go with the fish, meat or game, no sending out 100 portions of mixed veg and another 100 portions of mashed and roast potatoes. To this day I feel there was never better food served in all of Ireland. Michel had shown me really good food, introduced me to ways of cooking and the best of produce that were in another world from turkey and ham and mash. But Tim was the first chef who really inspired me.

Here was a kindred spirit. We cooked for footballers, actors and politicians—you name them, they came to Renvyle House. Richard Harris stayed there while he was filming the movie *The Field*. I met him and Brenda Fricker—all the stars. Sometimes I stayed in Kylemore in Nancy Naughton's B&B. She's a fantastic cook—she used to make her own sausages and black pudding—we used to spend all day talking about food.

I did two whole seasons in Renvyle House and it was one of the happiest times of my life. Tim's still head chef there and now one of my long-time greatest friends. I spent some time in Ballinahinch Castle too, where I learned to fish.

Later that first year I represented Renvyle House Hotel in a cooking competition in Dublin. Tim came to the school to help train me. I competed in six events and came home with four golds, an award for excellence and best overall winner. The media picked it up so it was all over the papers and I was invited on to afternoon television.

Tim O'Sullivan, one of the great Irish chefs

Bright lights calling

After the two years in Killybegs and the seasons in Renvyle I knew I'd have to leave Ireland. My mother could see that I needed to break that mould and start the next chapter. 'Surely you've learned enough now,' she said, 'it's time to move on. You can't be staying here forever, doing all the other chefs' work, and they getting all the credit.' She didn't want me to go up to Dublin at that stage—it would just have been turkey and ham again. The few times she was up in Dublin, going to a football match with my father, she went to the Green Isle Hotel or the Burlington, and she could see that I'd end up doing the stuff I'd been doing in Bundoran, the only difference would be the lifestyle. And of course at that stage I couldn't wait to leave Donegal—being young and arrogant I thought it had little to offer—it had no 5-star hotels! Nowadays I think it's the most fantastic place in the world, with one of the top hotels in the country, the Lough Eske Castle outside Donegal Town.

There was only one place for me to go—New York. There was a kind of a food revolution starting there at the time and I'd heard about French chefs doing wonderful things. The Americans staying in Renvyle House used to bring food magazines with them—*Gourmet, Condé Nast Traveller* and *Food and Wine*—I read them all. I can still remember looking at the photographs and thinking 'I want to learn to do this kind of food.' I already had a collection of cookbooks (whenever anybody asked me what I wanted for Christmas it was always 'A cookbook—Anton Mosiman, Paul Bocuse' and my mother would go down to Woods on Main Street in Letterkenny and they'd order them in) and my brother Keith used to send back menus from restaurants in the States. He was already over there in Boston and used to tell us every week about the amazing restaurants he'd eaten in, especially the ethnic ones. And the Americans had told me that you could make a fortune in New York . . .

The first time I saw my father cry was the day his mother died. I was four years old at the time but I'll always remember his face. The second time was the day he drove me to Dublin Airport.

Chapter 4
'The Irish chef'

I'LL NEVER FORGET THE HEAT at JFK—you could smell the humidity in the air. It was September 1988 and I was seventeen. I had flown over with a friend of mine, Paul Harvey, who was going to the States at the same time.

Keith met us off the plane. He'd been making $200 a week as an engineer in construction while his friends were making $300 a night working behind bars. 'Feck this,' he said, 'I'll come to New York. What's the point of slaving on a site all day when you can work in a bar, have a few drinks and there are lots of girls?' For the first couple of days I stayed in the YMCA then Keith got a job in The Blarney Stone, an Irish bar in Chelsea. The apartment above it came with the job, so the two of us moved in, along with two other Donegal guys who worked in the bar.

The first thing we'd see coming out onto the street every day was a line of hookers who worked right outside the apartment. But we weren't fazed, we talked to them every day until it got to the stage where they'd say 'Hey Irish! How'ya doin'?' Every Sunday when I woke up and looked out there'd be homeless people sleeping all over the streets. I knew it was time to leave when one morning I came out and there was a guy having a dump on the doorstep. We moved to Queens, which was a real Irish district then. But I loved Chelsea and whenever I went back to New York I always stayed there.

My first job

I had no job set up when I first arrived—there was no point even trying without a visa. I'd entered the lottery for a Donnelly visa but hadn't got one, so then I'd applied for a Morrison visa, but I hadn't heard anything yet. It was clear that the best thing to do would be to go to an Irish neighbourhood, get a job in an Irish restaurant and learn the lie of the land until the visa was sorted. So I just walked into a few Irish bars and told them I was a chef and was looking for a job. Usually I was fobbed off; I'd get 'Go and speak to this guy' or 'The boss is not here, come back later.' Then in one place they told me to speak to the Jones brothers—'They're expanding a lot'.

The Joneses were known for Jones Oil, their family business back in Ireland. They were smart guys with a lot of style, always in designer suits with gorgeous girls on their arms and wads of cash in their pockets. They also ran a construction company with a guy called Eddie Drivinghawke, a full-blooded Native American, as well as restaurants and bars, and were very successful and very money-driven.

I went to their flagship bar and restaurant, Blue Street, in a well-to-do Irish neighbourhood in Queens and they offered me a job as a chef. They served traditional Irish food, corned beef and cabbage, Irish stew—that kind of thing, After a few days there, doing just five covers for lunch and five for dinner, I went to the manager. 'Look—this isn't working. I want to change the menus.

It's no reflection on the food in Ireland but I want to put together a proper menu.' I started using ingredients that were unheard of for an Irish restaurant—goat's cheese, sun-dried tomatoes, pesto—and we were the first restaurant to do proper homemade Guinness bread. I was killing the suppliers, pushing them to the limit on quality. In Renvyle we used to get our fish fresh off the boat and I wanted the same standards in Blue Street.

Very quickly it got a name for good food and takings in the restaurant overtook those in the bar. Before long, you couldn't get a table there for three or four weeks and on Thursdays, Fridays and Saturdays it was always booked out. The restaurant was written about in the Irish-American papers—the *Irish Voice* and the *Irish Echo*—and even the Irish living in the Bronx and Manhattan came out to eat there. I started to build a reputation as 'the Irish chef'.

The other Irish guys I knew all worked in bars and wanted to drink and meet girls, but I was on a different mission. The celebrity chef thing was just getting going and I was starting to get serious. While my friends partied, I was preparing for my future. I signed up at New York University for a course in hotel management—housekeeping, purchasing, restaurant service, front of house etc.—and on my days off I used to go to the finest hotels in the city—the Waldorf, the Plaza and the Pierre—asking to do a *stage*. Usually what you do at these big hotels is you just turn up at the kitchen door, and they give you an application form to fill out. But even with my qualifications and experience, without a visa they wouldn't even let me fill out the form.

Then I got lucky, twice. Not only was I successful in the Morrison visa lottery, but one night the Executive Banqueting Chef from the Plaza, Joe Friel, came in to eat at Blue Street. He was from Donegal and he had been in the States for twenty years. His mother lived in the neighbourhood and she'd said to him 'Come on, you must try this little place here'. After the meal, he gave me his card and asked me to come for an interview for a job at the Plaza, which had recently been transformed by the millions Donald and Ivana Trump had spent on it. At that stage I still had a few hurdles to jump for the Morrison but of course I didn't let on.

I was offered a job in The Edwardian Room, the Plaza's three star fine dining restaurant. They'd had 71 applicants

In New York aged twenty

for the job, including French and Americans—for an Irish guy to get it was unheard of. But it turned out the executive chef—a Frenchman who cared only for food, fishing and his Porsche—loved to visit Ireland and loved the Irish people, so I had an advantage. On the day of the interview Anthony Quinn had been in to introduce his latest squeeze to the head chef, Brooke Shields and her mother were paying their bill at the reception and the waiters had got into a tizzy because Al Pacino had just come in and they didn't have a table. Obviously I wanted the job.

There were still a few problems—first was the Green Card. I still had to go back to Dublin, have a medical in the Blackrock Clinic, go up to the American embassy, do an interview, have my fingerprints taken, sign the forms and all of that. But luckily, it came through just in time.

Another problem was the starting salary at the Plaza—it would barely cover the rent. I told my brother I'd been offered a job as chef de partie 'whatever the fuck that is—but it's only $25,000 a year. After rent and bills there's nothing left.' My brother liked going to good restaurants, he enjoyed the whole buzz of fine food and wine, and good service skills, and the two of us would eat in the nice places and criticise them. He'd say to me: 'You could do better than that.' So he said 'Just do it. Do it for a year. It'll be your platform to move to the next thing. Don't worry about the numbers—I'll look after that.'

Then there were the Joneses. I didn't want to leave them in the lurch. I got on great with them and always spoiled them when they came to eat, so I really didn't want to do that. I told them about the job at the Plaza and of course they were disappointed, so I offered them a deal. They had a huge Irish place in the Bronx called Beechers where they had about 400 people for lunch on Sundays. The Edwardian Room was closed on Sundays and Mondays so I could work for the Joneses on my days off. I said 'I'll do it if you give me $600 a day. I'll do it all myself. I'll get in at seven in the morning, I'll leave at twelve at night, I don't need any help. And on Mondays I'll work at one of your other places—help you with menus and all that.'

And they agreed. I ended up with a little enterprise, spending a couple of mornings here and a couple of mornings there. I was working for the Joneses, writing menus, training staff and finding chefs and consulting at various places. I trained Mexicans to cook the food— they're really good workers, hungry like the Irish. So all my time at the Plaza and later at the Waldorf Astoria I worked for nearly half a dozen Irish restaurants on top of everything else. I was like a machine in those days, wanting to work all the time.

The Plaza

I'll never forget the day I walked into the Plaza's main kitchen—it was absolutely huge, the size of a football pitch and there were all these white hats. There were 160 chefs in the hotel. I was thrown in at the deep end, straight into The Edwardian Room. It had its own kitchen, off the main one. There were different sections with chefs de partie in each one, managed by a chef tournant. I was put in the starter section. Then I moved onto fish, then meat. I started at 6.45 a.m. and finished at 3.15 p.m., back at 5 p.m. and worked all the way through to 11.30.

I felt at home immediately, Joe Friel became an instant drinking buddy and a good friend to this day. I was someone he could talk to about the old country and he would school me on the American way.

On my first evening Don Johnson and Melanie Griffith were at the chef's table about three feet from where I was working. It was fashionable at the time to have a table in the kitchen for star guests—the celebrities loved it, because they were away from the public, and they felt they were getting special treatment. We didn't change our ways for them—there was plenty of shouting but of course they liked that too—the drama, the entertainment. The first celebrity meal I prepared was a smoked duck salad with portobello mushrooms, baby spinach salad and raspberry dressing. When I told the guys back in the apartment that I was cooking for the stars they thought I was lying—they thought I should have been washing dishes on my first day.

I spent the next few months learning the menu, developing my management skills, having melons thrown at me because they weren't ripe enough, getting screamed at by everybody from the head waiter to the executive chef, from the chefs de partie to the food and beverage manager. I soon learned the politics of a huge hotel where the blame was always passed down and down along the line.

On my third day there, Donald Trump came in for lunch and ordered a shrimp cocktail. I was asked to make it, but when I smelled the shrimp I thought they weren't fresh enough. I wanted to use only the best shrimp, drizzle some lemon juice on them and grind a little black pepper over them. I shouted to the chef, 'Permission to go to the storeroom, Chef—we need some fresh shrimp, these aren't great.' But the chef wouldn't let me go as he was under pressure. 'Fast, Gallagher! Just serve them, they're OK.' I said, 'Fine—if that's what you want.'

Two minutes later the shrimp cocktail came back to the kitchen. All the powers that be—the executive chef, the food and beverage manager, the president of the hotel—landed in the kitchen and started yelling at me—'These shrimp are off!' I was told to pack my things and go downstairs to the union office to be fired. Ten minutes later the chef confessed that it was his fault, not mine, that I had said that the shrimp were not fresh and under pressure he had ignored me. So I was reinstated.

A month later I was moved up the ranks to chef tournant and six months later I was promoted to sous chef. I was only twenty years old. The head chef now felt he could leave me in charge of the whole kitchen. He would come in and give out a bit, change a few things so that everybody would know that he was still the king, go around all the tables and check on the guests and then leave to live the playboy lifestyle he was so famous for, leaving me to take care of the restaurant. I was in no rush home; home was a two-bedroom apartment with six people sharing.

One night Donald Trump came in again for dinner. All he wanted was a steak cooked plain, no fancy sauces and some sautéed potatoes. I jumped at the chance to impress. I cut the best steak I could find, seasoned it up nicely, got some olive oil, confit of garlic, unsalted butter and cooked and basted the most perfect steak I had ever cooked. He ordered it rare, and rare it was. I handled it with love and care—there was no way this guy was not going to enjoy it. I assembled the sautéed potatoes in a little pile, placed the nice 14 oz sirloin steak on the centre of the plate and poured a little of the confit garlic basting juice on top. Then I brought it to the passe for the waiter to take out to Trump.

Every time the restaurant manager came into the kitchen—every 20 seconds—I'd ask him 'Is he eating? Is he smiling? Did he say anything?' About 30 minutes later, Trump asked to see the chef who'd cooked his steak. I froze. Did he not like it? Was he going to yell at me? I turned my apron around to the clean side and marched out to the dining room to get my trashing. The captain (the head waiter) introduced me:

'Excuse me, Mr Trump. This is the man who cooked your steak.'

'What's your name, son?'

'Conrad Gallagher.'

'Are you British?'

'No, I'm Irish.'

'In all my years I have never tasted a better steak. How did you cook it?"

'I just showed it the love, Mr Trump.'

Every single time I met him after that he remembered my name. 'Conrad, how are you? Keep up the good work.'

A few weeks later there was a March and Dimes Cook Off at the Plaza, where celebrities came and cooked with different chefs to raise money for charity. I was teamed up with Demi Moore and Bruce Willis and it was my first real taste of red carpet celebrity. I'd seen the celebrities at the chef's table but this was the first time I'd been face to face with them. The whole event was hosted by Joan Rivers and televised live. I was interviewed about my two's ability to cook and I came out with a beautiful one liner. 'If I was Bruce Willis and Demi Moore was my wife, I'd learn how to cook' and all my comrades cheered.

I worked up a reputation as a grafter. I had no problem coming in at six in the morning and staying till twelve at night. I wasn't a militant union guy, I never complained, I was happy just to work away. And I was hungry. So as well as working for the Joneses and the other Irish bars I started doing *stages* at different places. (One was with Daniel Boulud at Le Cirque, and later I worked with him in his own place. He was doing fusion stuff—classic and nouvelle with Asian influences, it was really exciting and intense and he was always trying new things—sometimes in the middle of service.) I was definitely a guy that top places felt they could hire easily—they could see I was a hard worker.

By this time I'd made a lot of contacts and good Irish-American friends just by going round the tables and talking to people. I also joined the New York Junior Culinary Team, which brought us all around the country, competing against other cities. I became captain of the team and we won four national medals. I was driving a jeep, dating—life was good. I used to do consultancy for different Irish gin mills around New York and catering for christenings and weddings.

I was one of the team for Eddie Murphy's wedding at the Plaza. There were 500 or 600 at it and I'll never forget when I was carving the Beef Wellington, this star basketball player came up with a most beautiful super-model and she asked me what the dish was and I said 'It's Beef Wellington with a red wine sauce' and she kept saying to me 'Will you say it again?'—she loved my accent so much. Within ten minutes there was this crew of Bronx residents in a line around me getting me to talk about the menu over and over. That was my first glimpse of how I could use my accent to my advantage.

At this stage I felt I was well on my way, that I was becoming a good chef, with respect for my produce and a good leader. My downfall was a temper. It not only scared me but most likely most of the union because when I lost it you could have heard me for miles and the chain of command didn't matter. If the general manager or Trump himself had been in front of me I would have fucked them from a height. Be it bad food, overcooked fish or anything that didn't meet my standards I lost it, screaming and shouting, going into overdrive, throwing things around and breaking plates. There's always huge pressure in a restaurant kitchen—you'll have maybe hundreds of diners, all choosing different combinations of meals, all cooked to order, everyone at a table having to be served at the same time, never mind what they're having, so getting the timing right is a battle every time. You'll have people screaming at each other 'Is that fucking sauce ready? Where are the mushrooms? Move it with the duck—the scallops are ready to go!' It's noisy, it's hot, you're trying to concentrate on what you're doing, to do the best job you can and then if something goes wrong you feel let down and the roaring starts . . .

CONRAD GALLAGHER

Moving on—The Waldorf

Donald Trump began to have money trouble, we never saw him much anymore, the Gulf War started, business was tough, nobody was leaving their jobs and the prospect for me of becoming top dog of the kitchen started to become distant. So I was ready for another challenge.

One evening in 1992, the food and beverage manager of the Waldorf Astoria, Howard Karp, was having a drink in the Jameson Bar on 51st and 2nd Avenue, where my brother Keith was the bartender. *Gourmet Magazine* had just written up The Edwardian Room and there was a picture in it of the Plaza head chef and me. My proud brother showed Karp the picture and the article in which my boss had praised me for my devotion and hard work.

A few days later I got a phone call from human resources at the Waldorf. They wanted me in for an interview. They'd invested $20 million in their restaurant, Peacock Alley, which was due to reopen shortly after renovations, and had just hired a hot young chef—Laurent Manrique from Gascony who could apparently cook like a god and they wanted somebody young and skilled to be his sous chef.

I had an interview with the executive chef John Doherty—he was of Irish descent, and we were to become great friends—and then I had a cook-off. They gave me a basket of produce: lovely sea bass, pearl onions, balsamic vinegar, a lobster and peppers. I remember doing a very simple lobster salad and pepper stew with a poached quail's egg on top, blanching off the little onions and adding fresh citrus juice and loads of fresh coriander. I seasoned the sea bass with sea salt and pepper and seared it off in a little olive oil. When the plate came in I could see John Doherty's eyes lighting up. And I made a crème brûlée and of course I didn't know the ovens but the custard was perfect and then I caramelised the top. He tried to crack it but it was a lovely brittle caramel and I knew then I had the job.

I started work as sous chef at Peacock Alley a month later. We had a week to build the team and get to know Laurent before the restaurant reopened. Laurent spoke very little English at that time but between my kitchen French and his broken English we managed.

Laurent understood the value of the complete dining experience—the food, the wine, the service, the ambience —he was one of the most demanding chefs I ever worked with. As far as he was concerned the food came first and foremost, he would not attend any meetings, he didn't want to know about protocols and procedures, that was my job. I was the sous chef, the commander in the kitchen so as well as the eighteen hours in the kitchen, I dealt with the bureaucracy and all the usual hassle, the compliance issues, the politics. Laurent never worried about budgets—a bad habit I picked up from him.

Within two months of Laurent constantly standing over my shoulder I had forgotten everything I had ever learned about food—all my classical training was out the window. He wanted me to start from zero. He changed my style, my thinking, my temperament and my attitude. I saw cooking and food in a whole different way. I had never seen food from the Basque region before—it was bright and colourful, with lots of braising and techniques

The Waldorf Astoria, New York

*Peacock Alley at the Waldorf Astoria, where I was Sous Chef
at twenty-one years old*

that were new to me, and huge powerful flavours. He'd use fresh black truffles, take unusual cuts of meat—shin, gizzard, heart—and do wonderful things with them. We did braised lamb shank with roasted potatoes, confit tomatoes and parsley, pumpkin soup with braised veal shank, little crabmeat and beetroot salads and every type of foie gras terrine you can think of.

Laurent's flavours would hit you with a punch. It was the skill he had to bring out the flavours, not just the braising and the slow cooking, it was much more than that—this was the best food I had ever tasted or had ever seen. I learned more under him than I had learned in my whole career so far.

Laurent did not take criticism well and always did exactly what he wanted. He became quite famous in a short period of time and got lots of press and TV coverage. I was his sidekick and protégé, always standing beside him. But the better I became, the cockier I got. At that time there was a lot of politics in the hotel. We were seen as different from the rest of the staff, we were the prima donnas. We never gave a thought to budget, food costs (we flew in food from France every day and used foie gras and truffles in everything) or staffing costs (we had 30 chefs to do 60 covers) and closed two days a week. Even our appearance was arrogant. I had long hair, never wore hats and wore the finest Bragard jackets, which had to be dry-cleaned, while everybody else wore heavy starched jackets.

One of the staff was a man with a serious cocaine addiction who drank about 30 coffees a day and ate rare steaks. I always found him a liability to be around. We exchanged words at the beginning of my time there and they would be the last pleasant words between us. Memos were great in those days—'Send me a fucking memo asshole,' I would say to him and off he would go complaining to Laurent because I was rude to him. He was up and down like a yo-yo. This was the first time I had seen cocaine in the restaurant business. From that time on I knew drugs and the restaurant business didn't mix. You can do what you want on the outside, but taking a hyper person, giving him coke and putting him in a stressful environment is lethal. I saw it first hand.

It was at the Waldorf that I met my good friend, Guy Kellner, who came as food and beverage manager, and Eric Long who came as general manager. They were hired to make profits but I was there to learn about great food and I didn't want to be bothered about gross profits or wage costs. One guy I remember from that time was the manager's assistant Chris, a French Canadian. He and I aspired to be the next team—me in the back and him front of house.

Unfortunately, by the time I went looking for him, he had settled down with a wife and kids, and gone for the calmer option of being manager of a hotel in Canada. I thought it was such a waste of talent! The thing is, some people just want happy families, they don't want the lifestyle of working late at night. And it's hard for your partner when she's home five or six nights a week by herself and you finish work at twelve. Then when you're younger, there's the whole rock 'n' roll lifestyle as well. It's different for me now, but at that age when we finished work at midnight, we didn't want to go to bed, so we'd end up in a pub or nightclub till five or six in the morning. So it's very difficult to be a family man, because when Sunday comes, you just want to veg. These days of course, that's exactly what I am, but back then when I was young and hungry, I didn't understand it.

I was becoming the top Irish chef in New York, so every time *Good Morning America* wanted someone to come on to cook corned beef and cabbage they'd ask me. Or if Gerry Adams, say, was coming to town and there was a gala dinner on at the hotel, I'd be the one invited to do it. Or if there was an Irish event like St Patrick's Day. Presidents have always stayed in the Waldorf Astoria when they're in New York. Their organisers, staff, security people and assistants spend a lot of their time in the kitchen, because they come in through the passageways. So when President Clinton wanted someone to cook the dinner at the White House for his first St Patrick's Day it made sense that he would take someone from the Waldorf. As I was the Irish chef there and I'd got to know a few of them, including some very powerful Irish Americans, I was the natural choice. It was arranged I would do *Good Morning America* that St Patrick's morning, cook the corned beef and cabbage, then I would fly up to the White House and prepare the dinner.

The White House had a French chef and its whole team was superb. The St Patrick's dinner took six weeks to organise. I devised the menu—I remember it included quail cooked over a turf fire with the turf flown in from Ireland. I'd write out the menus, send them over, the White House would come back with queries, I'd send them back, and so on, and the whole time I couldn't say a word to anybody as it had to be kept hush hush for security reasons. There were about 80 people at the dinner including Taoiseach Albert Reynolds. I wasn't nervous—at that stage I was used to meeting big names.

The best chefs in the world would come to dine in the Waldorf, all the three-star Michelin masters. Laurent would eat with them and I would cook and serve them and meet them. They were all astonished that I wasn't French: the fact that I was Irish puzzled them. 'Is your mother French?' they would ask. To make them feel better, sometimes I would say 'No, she's German.' They all invited me to France to study under them but I felt it was too soon. When I was about sixteen I'd done a *stage* with Paul Bocuse for a week in Lyon but I was too young and I got very little out of it, it made very little impression. So I knew the timing had to be right.

Then one day Laurent told me that Alain Ducasse was coming in the next day and he was going to eat with him, 'So you can do us a nice little tasting menu'. Ducasse was the youngest chef ever to win three Michelin stars and the first to earn six stars. At that time he was head chef at the Louis XV in the Hotel de Paris in Monte Carlo. People would fly in from all over the world just to have dinner there. He and Laurent sat at the back of the restaurant at around nine or ten p.m., and I did a lovely four-course tasting menu for them. Ducasse must have been impressed because he said he was coming back in a month to do dinner at the Pierre Hotel for four days and he wanted me to assist him. Rumour had it he was being paid £20,000 a day, flying in twenty chefs and all his ingredients on Concorde.

I organised the logistics of the whole thing: 'This is how we're going to do it: the ingredients will be here, that walk-in fridge here for this, five guys work here, five guys work there, I'll brief the waiters, you take care of the captain, I'll make sure the ingredients are done on this day', all the details of who was to do what, from the schedules and briefings to how long the lobster needed to be cooked. The publicity from the event was huge. I gained great experience and of course brownie points from Ducasse—'Laurent's Irish boy working for me for free—ah!'

He was obviously happy, because when it was over, he gave me an open invitation to go to Monte Carlo. By that stage I'd been at the Waldorf for a year and a half so it felt right. Laurent told me he wanted me to do it. His idea was that I'd work for Ducasse for a year, then come back to work for him as he would have his own restaurant by then.

I was meant to go in September, but the Waldorf wouldn't release me as my contract ran till January. So on Stephen's Day 1993 I flew straight to France from New York and started work in Monte Carlo two days later.

The next year was one of the loneliest of my life.

Chapter 5
Time to do my own thing

LEAVING NEW YORK WAS TOUGH. I might have had the skills and the knowledge for Monte Carlo, and maybe more determination than most, but I was leaving a lot behind. I had a network of people in New York—my brother, Laurent—and all the friends I had made and the contacts I had built up. But in Monte Carlo I knew nobody. For the first time in my life I felt lonely and insecure.

Plus I was short of money. I had my plane fare and my last two weeks' wages, $800, but that was going to last about two seconds in a town where a coffee and a croissant can cost $20. I had to live off my savings because I'd be working for room and board only, which was a basement room in the hotel shared with five others.

The restaurant was the Louis XV in the five-star Hotel de Paris, a few steps from the casino and the sea. The dining room glitters there's so much gold in it—on the plates, the chairs, the walls—it really is like eating in the king's palace. The chef de cuisine, Laurent Gras, ran the kitchen for Ducasse. At that stage, there was a two-year waiting list for a chef's position there. There were 40 chefs in the kitchen to do 60 covers and half of them were working for free. The man himself wasn't around all that much—he was looking after his other interests, promoting his cookbooks and building his brand. But we were there six days a week, sixteen hours a day—twelve hours cooking, four hours cleaning. And if you wanted to learn pastry and baking you had to do it on your day off.

There hadn't been a non-French speaker there in twelve years, let alone an Irish non-speaker—it was unheard of. So I was christened 'Ireland' and given the dirty jobs to start with, so it was back to peeling potatoes. 'If you don't like it go back to Ireland' the French guys would say to me. But I felt confident I could cook better than any of them if I was given the chance.

I learned an awful lot from Ducasse—the importance of discipline, the need for perfection in every aspect of a restaurant, not just the cooking, but the best service, the best management, the best produce.

I soon took over a section, but it was only for three months. They insisted on that to ensure that you stayed your full year. If you wanted the recipes for that section you had to work that section—it was the only way to get to know how they were done. The recipes were too complicated to remember easily—but Ducasse wouldn't give them out and he told the top guys not to be giving them out. You'd have to try to write them down in secret. There was no point in relying on the top chefs' cookbooks, you'd never be able to reproduce their great dishes using their books.

To top it all, Ducasse's approach was completely different from Manrique's. Everything I did was wrong! So I had to retrain all over again. Ducasse's style was subtle and sophisticated. Where Manrique's flavours were powerful, Ducasse's were delicate. Manrique would use

French haute cuisine: forty chefs worked in Alain Ducasse's kitchen supplying sixty covers in the Restaurant Louis XV in the Hotel de Paris, Monte Carlo. I was twenty-three and learned a lot, but working there was one of the loneliest times of my life.

ox cheek, Ducasse would use fillet steak. Where Laurent would meld flavours Ducasse would cook ingredients separately and only combine them at the end. But if you asked me to choose between them, who was the better chef, I'd say Manrique.

I did a whole season in Monte Carlo, working away very aggressively. It was work, sleep, work, sleep. The only time we saw daylight was on our day off—when we came out we'd be rubbing our eyes—that's how bad it was. We were so tired we didn't want to do anything in our free time except lie around—anyway, we had no money. By December, after a year of it, I was exhausted. I was twenty-three, I'd cooked at a serious level under a lot of serious people, my head was getting muddled with it all.

By that stage I'd probably seen enough anyway. I felt I understood Ducasse's style. It was like engineering, he could change the ingredients as much as he liked—from sea bass with artichokes and lobster sauce to braised veal shank with confit of tomatoes and zucchini blossoms—but I knew his philosophy. I felt I'd got as much as I was going to get from him and I wasn't going anywhere.

Back to Ireland

I was due to stay in Monte Carlo till June but something told me I wouldn't. Over the years while I was away I got phone calls and job offers, including one from the K Club, maybe because Michael Smurfit was honorary consul to Monaco while I was there. I was also becoming well known in Ireland—there had been stuff in the papers at home about me in the White House, cooking for the President, captaining the culinary team and winning medals. I was also hugely ambitious. And the year with Ducasse made me realise that I didn't have to be the one doing all the work for someone else who sat on his arse and took all the credit. My friends and family said it too: 'Jaysus, you've worked for these guys long enough. It's about time you came home and made some dosh.'

I was also poorer than ever. I went home to Donegal for Christmas and my father had to send me the money for the ticket home. In France, I couldn't even go out for a pint. I was sick of it. I wanted a nice home and a nice car. No more jeans, taking trains and living on a budget. I'd had enough of that.

I went down to Dublin, had a good look around and

ate in a few restaurants. The standard of food was nowhere close to what I'd been doing in Monte Carlo and New York. The first person I met was Michael Fitzgerald who owned The Commons on Stephen's Green. I had a chat with him. He had a Michelin star at the time and maybe had aspirations to have another one. But his style was classic, very different to mine, and I wasn't sure I could work with him. Then I met Alan O'Reilly of Morels. He owned Clarets in Blackrock. He was a fantastic chef and we instantly hit it off. He became a great friend— he always managed to squeeze in a phone call to me when times were tough. Alan told me he needed a chef for Morels. I told him I'd do it for three to six months. I figured I could make my mark on the place pretty quickly and go back to New York in the Spring with some money in my pocket.

Morels was in rooms over the Eagle House pub in Glasthule in south Dublin, near the sea. I went out, looked around, looked at the service and decided to do upmarket French bistro—daubes of beef, lamb shanks, rabbit—stuff people weren't doing then. And it was a huge success, within three weeks it was packed to the doors. There was a real buzz about it. The food critics really liked it, they loved the Mediterranean style, the food wasn't too rich, there were no heavy sauces with loads of cream and butter. I was using olive oil, peppers, garlic and rocket salad.

There was another sort of publicity too when I fired six chefs in six weeks. But I've never liked clock watchers and I'm not very tolerant of people who don't give of their best. I don't mind someone who doesn't know the proper way to slice vegetables, or make a sauce, as long as they're willing to learn. I don't mind teaching people and I'll always have the time and patience to show staff the way I want something done. But I go insane if I catch people taking shortcuts just because my back is turned for a minute. Staff learn very quickly with me that there is nothing I don't see and if they take shortcuts I will throw out their work and make them start again. You don't get two chances in a restaurant—the food has to be perfect first time around or else you'll have a very dissatisfied customer.

My own place

I stayed on in Morels after St Patrick's Day. Then one day I was chatting to Derry Clarke of L'Ecrivain restaurant, which at that time was in Baggot Street. He said 'By the way, I'm moving this week.' He was moving L'Ecrivain up the road to a bigger place. I asked him then what he was doing with the old restaurant and he said the lease was available.

This was my chance. After all the years of working for other chefs I had an opportunity to have the name Conrad Gallagher over the door. I felt I was ready and I wanted it. So I went for it.

Now, in hindsight, I ask myself how different things might have been. I could have stayed on with Ducasse until the following June and then returned to New York to work with Manrique. Up to that point I'd done everything right and it wasn't a natural progression for me to come back to Ireland and set up my own place. I'd spent six years slogging in New York and Monte Carlo and I'd earned my own pedigree—the Plaza, the Waldorf, Le Cirque, Ducasse. I could have gone back to New York, become head chef or executive chef in a restaurant or hotel and earned $300,000 a year, making my own reputation and winning my own stars.

I don't know what happened, really; maybe I was just restless. I seemed to get caught up in Ireland. Maybe I just wanted a break, I'd been away for so long. It wasn't the pressure. When you're young you're well able for pressure. Looking back, I probably should have kept going for another while and worked for a few more people. But that's that—I can't change it now.

The premises weren't ideal, they were in a basement and were really small—we could only do 40 covers, but I was keen to get going. It was a two-year landlord lease. I was paid very well in Morels and had saved about £5,000 or £6,000 and my dad gave me £7,500 and I managed to raise the rest one way or another. I called it Peacock Alley, after the famous restaurant in New York that taught me so much.

I very quickly got a great young team together. I was only twenty-four myself. We opened the doors on a Wednesday at the end of May 1995 and it never stopped. It was new and cutting edge—I called it 'A Taste of the Mediterranean'. The menu was quite short with things like crispy confit of duck—people had loved that in Morels—and crab salad with lemon confit, cilantro and beetroot, done in layers, and wild salmon coated in cous cous, with fondue of leeks or purée of squash, and napoleon of vegetables with layers of sautéed and puréed vegetables sandwiched between Parmesan tuiles. So there were a lot of different textures and tastes in every dish—crunchy, crispy, creamy and sharp. I wanted to bring out the flavours in the ingredients—which were always the very best I could find. And I loved to experiment and to mix flavours, so the food in Peacock Alley was always exciting.

Some people hated my cooking—they said it was too complicated. But most people loved it. The tradition says food should be simple but I don't see why food should be dull—food should be like Grand Opera—full of excitement and entertainment, with lots of big punchy flavours. I like different infusions of flavours, little oils, marmalades, onions and vinaigrettes. I don't like heavy sauces. A three-flavoured dish, starchy vegetables and a meat, I find quite boring to eat.

The cancer

One day, a few months after Peacock Alley opened—the lunch service had just finished—I decided I'd better do something about a lump I'd felt on my testicle. It wasn't a lump that you could ignore, it was getting to the stage where it was taking over with the pain. I walked down the road to the outpatients' clinic at Baggot Street Hospital and told the doctor I had a pain in my . . . It was really embarrassing. He said, 'Sit up on the table there and drop your trousers'. And then very quickly: 'Can you go down to the Meath straight away—there's an oncologist down there—he'll have a look at it for you.'

I got a taxi and by the time I got to the Meath Hospital there were three doctors waiting at the door for me. I was brought for a CAT scan, and next thing they were telling me 'You've got a tumour and we have to remove it tomorrow.'

When I woke up after the surgery I was missing a testicle. I was told I'd have to have chemotherapy and radiotherapy and it was very unlikely I'd ever be a father.

I sat in the hospital for three or four days. Luckily, Gavin O'Rourke was my head chef at the time (he stayed with me for seven years) and he was able to manage the kitchen and the team kept everything going for me—they were great.

After the surgery they gave me a week or two for the wounds to heal and then I started the most excruciating therapies—chemotherapy and radiation. It was all done in St Luke's Hospital, in Rathgar. Every day at 3.15 they'd put in an intravenous drip. For a long time if I had to drive anywhere in Rathmines or through Milltown or up in that area I'd always try to avoid driving up Highfield Road, past the hospital entrance.

It was a really bad winter that year, it rained all the time and I remember the days were dark when I went up to Rathgar for treatment. And of course the treatment makes you throw up. They offered me anti-nausea tablets but the problem is that if you take them you don't actually vomit but you feel sick and you go on feeling sick. But if you don't take them you get sick and then it's over with. My uncle Eamon, who was doorman in Peacock Alley at the time, used to drive me back and forth to the hospital; we'd be at the gates of St Luke's after the treatment, and I'd have a bucket between my legs, I'd vomit into it, then it was home to my flat in Stillorgan, shower, change and get back to the restaurant by a quarter to seven. The vomiting would have passed but the headaches would be excruciating from all the toxins in my head. By half ten or eleven my temperature would be high, my lips would be really red, my mouth would be dry and I'd be in shit form. I used to go straight home to bed and then I suffered from the shivers and all sorts of stuff, but with any luck I'd wake up fine the next morning.

I had twenty sessions of chemo. The radiation was just as bad. It was given straight into the stomach—I used to feel really sick from it. the staff were great in St Luke's, but it was hard to keep your spirits up, especially when there were young kids and old people there.

After the treatment, I was given the all clear.

Spreading my wings

Peacock Alley's reputation kept growing and growing. There was quite a bit of hype around it, like Morels, and people who'd eaten there followed me to Baggot Street. It very quickly got to the stage where you couldn't book a Saturday night for five or six weeks. I knew I had to get a bigger place, Baggot Street was just too small. Managing the bookings was costing me a fortune in administration. Back in those days people would book tables and then not show up, cancelling at the last minute. So I took a deposit by credit card for bookings of six or more and warned people that if they didn't show up I'd charge them. Peacock Alley was the first restaurant in Ireland to do that. Of course, people complained but it was great publicity. I went on a radio show and had a little tantrum. I said 'Look—if you book a seat on an airline and you don't show up you get charged, if you book a table and you don't show up I'll lose that sitting.'

My uncle Frankie always said to me 'You'll never make any money in that place, you're hot at the moment, you need to strike while the going is good.' So I asked a family friend from Donegal, Brian Magill, to keep an eye out for a place for me.

'I need to find somewhere bigger—it's scandalous the amount of bookings I'm turning away, it's not big enough, I just can't get the turnover. I turned every table three times on Saturday.'

He told me about a place on South William Street called Café Caruso; it was run by Rhona Teehan but she wanted to move on. I heard about it on a Monday, had a look at it and saw that it needed a lot of work—but other than that it was perfect. So I went back the next day with my accountant and said to Rhona 'Let's do a deal'. She asked when I wanted to move in and I said

Peacock Alley, South William Street, Dublin 1996–98

'Next Monday.' The lease was £150,000. She was looking for £75,000 down payment but she agreed to stagger it. I still had to get the landlord's agreement so I drove down to his home in Galway on the Sunday and we started renovations the following Monday.

Some of my family came down from Donegal and it was all done really fast—it took a couple of weeks. The kitchen was completely redone with new equipment, lighting, stainless steel and tiling—it cost £40,000. We had a separate bar with comfortable sofas. We just had so much more room, I had an office upstairs, and there was a laundry room. The main room had a huge skylight which gave it a nice airy feeling; the walls were painted in dark colours and that showed off the paintings—I had an interest in modern Irish art and started building a collection by young Irish artists—bright, abstract paintings. And there was a huge copper coffee urn and a classical statue. I ordered the best Irish linen, cutlery from Newbridge, china from Villeroy and Boch, Riedel glasses, everything the best quality. And of course it all cost a fortune. The bank didn't want to know so I was having to rob Peter to pay Paul. I was repaying things on the drip—it was touch and go for a few months.

We closed Baggot Street on a Saturday in April 1996 and opened up in South William Street on the following Tuesday. We doubled the number of covers, to 80, and I doubled the staff—from 12 to 24—it was no problem because so many people wanted to work with me. I had to train the new ones to work my way, in sections. There was no set menu—we had à la carte and a tasting menu.

It was lift-off from day one. Every night was full, it

Inside the South William Street restaurant—my customers loved it, but it was just too small.

took about six weeks to get a Saturday night table and it became *the* place to entertain clients, so we did a lot of corporate and government business. We really had the right customer base. People would spend serious money and by Christmas I was able to pay everybody all I owed.

Through my good friend Tony Campbell I got into catering for some of the banks, including Anglo Irish Bank. We did three of their Christmas parties in a row (in South William Street and later when we moved to the Fitzwilliam Hotel). At one of these parties I left at 1.30 a.m. only to be called at 4 a.m. by one of the staff—they wanted to close the bar. There wasn't a cigar left and some of the guests had been drinking bottles of 1978 Lynch Bages by the neck. The bill had gone to £38,000.

South William Street was a fun restaurant, it was friendly—I bred that sort of personality. The waiters weren't too up with themselves, the manager wasn't

I started doing tall food in Peacock Alley. It's a presentation style, a kind of food architecture, that became a craze for a while. But you can't just fan a piece of lamb into a dozen slices and pile them on top of egg plant because when the waiter picks up the plate the tower will fall over. There's a lot of skill involved.

snooty and the wine waiter wasn't cocky. What happens in the first five minutes when you walk in the door is so important—so it had to be friendly first, the managers had to be pro customer, to recognise people, not to be intimidating and not to be condescending. If someone asked a question about the menu they had to explain it simply—I hammered all that home.

There'd always be some crisis to handle—the coffee machine not working, a tour company going bust owing me a packet, the game not arriving, break-ins, staff not turning up, bills not being paid. Costs were very hard to control. Glasses and plates were broken every service, wine was spilled on tablecloths. There was always drama, always hassle and always people leaving and coming. I was very easy to upset and I got a reputation for hiring and firing. I would freak if people wasted food. I came from a background where you just didn't do that—I could never forget Mrs McEniff taking me round the bins at the end of the day's service checking to see if the chefs had wasted any food. And it took a while for some suppliers to realise that I wouldn't accept poor produce. I always sourced the best ingredients—vegetables from France, crab meat from Castletownbere and handpicked herbs.

At first I used to spend my day shouting. Then I tried to shout before a mistake was made, rather than after. So many things can go wrong with food—sometimes things can be put right but often enough failures have to be binned and that's your profit down the drain.

There were always new staff to be trained and sometimes they'd do disastrous things just because they didn't know any better. I keep my mother dough in the main fridge—it's used for all the yeast bread. The bread is very important—a lot of bread served even in the best restaurants is too new. I don't mean that it shouldn't be baked fresh just before each service, it's that the mother dough is too fresh. When you make the bread, you keep, say, half a pound back and then the next time you make bread you add that, and you keep a bit of the new batch and so it goes on. And you could end up with some mother dough in the fridge that could be ten or twelve years old. The mother dough gives the bread more flavour,

Great bread has been a trademark of all my restaurants. If a customer leaves my lovely bread fresh out of the oven just sitting there I have to stop myself going up and saying 'Eat it now—it's warm!'

it makes a better bread.

Once when I was training in a new commis I asked him to clean out the fridge. He came back and said 'I found some stinking old gloop in the back—it looked like it'd been there for years.' I freaked—he'd thrown out the mother dough. So he had to grab some rubber gloves and overalls and climb into the bin and find it in among all the garbage. Another time I asked a trainee to strain the stockpot. He came back to me proudly with a heap of bones—the stock, which had been cooking for six hours, had gone down the sink.

South William Street was on its own journey—I kept pushing it, making it better and better. In those days I was never happy with anything I did, that was the breed of a perfectionist, obsessive person that I was. The tomatoes weren't red enough, sauces weren't smooth enough, bread wasn't crispy enough. Because I'd come from a three star Michelin background, nothing could ever be good enough. The presentation of the room was never quite right, the tablecloths were never ironed well enough, I had Villeroy and Boch plates but I wanted Bernardaud, I had silver cutlery but I wanted gold, I had 500 wines but I wanted 1000. That was the kind of person I was, always pushing, pushing, driven.

Even before moving to South William Street the media was getting as interested in my private life as my professional life. I had dated a couple of people in bands, Terry Keane had written about me and the social pages had an interest in what I was doing personally. I did a couple of episodes of *Gourmet Ireland*, and afternoon television at RTÉ with Thelma Mansfield and Marty Whelan.

BACK ON THE MENU

Two stars

Shortly after opening in South William Street I met Domini Kemp and very quickly we got together. She had just finished the cookery course at Leiths in London, and she wanted to learn, so she came in to the business, part time at first, as front of house. She hadn't done it before, but was well able for it and took care of the media and the reservations. We got engaged and started living together, in a rented flat first. We were working all hours—things were flying and we wanted to make the most of it. Then Domini got pregnant. We didn't expect that after the cancer so it was a great surprise. We bought a house in Rathfarnham and put in a top class kitchen—I couldn't cook in an ordinary kitchen, though to tell the truth I've never cooked that much at home, all I want at the end of the day's service is something really simple.

For a long time I'd wanted to write a cookbook—a book for people who love food, cooking and reading recipes so I decided 1997 was the year to do it. I can't even begin to describe how difficult it was. I thought it was finished and it was only starting. Getting the recipes onto paper was mainly Domini's job. As she's a chef I was able to explain to her what went into each dish, the ingredients and the way it was cooked. The first thing to do was to decide what recipes to include. I have hundreds of ideas going through my mind all the time of dishes I want to serve and different ways of making them. We wanted to put in dishes that would stand the test of time and customer favourites —like the daube of beef, the crab and beetroot salad—our customers used to go crazy if they weren't on the menu.

Then the testing and editing began. Domini put an awful lot of work into it. We'd sometimes disagree about what steps should be included or modified, as Domini would say she's a 'lazy' chef whereas I'm a perfectionist, I'd go to any lengths to create a perfect dish. We modified the recipes from how we did them in Peacock Alley for the domestic kitchen—getting home cooks to try them and then using their feedback to simplify the recipes while keeping them true. Walter Pfeiffer took the photographs of the food and Brian Daly the action ones in the restaurant. *New Irish Cooking—Recipes from Peacock Alley* was published in October 1997—we had a great launch in the restaurant, over 300 people came, and I went on the *Late Late Show* to talk about the book.

Lauren was born a few weeks later. That was one of the best things that ever happened to me—I am just so proud of her. Domini is a wonderful mother. She has done a great job bringing Lauren up.

When South William Street was open about a year, and we'd won various accolades, Restaurant of the Year, Chef of the Year, four AA rosettes, people kept saying that it'd be great to have a more casual Conrad Gallagher restaurant, with simpler food and cheaper. The La Scala on Merrion Street was available so I did a deal on it in March and we opened as Lloyds Brasserie in November. It flew from day one.

We closed for four or five days in January and went off to Adare Manor for a break because I'd been working really hard over Christmas. Then we came back and it was hell for leather again. We knew that the Michelin stars would be announced at the end of the month. In those days there weren't that many Michelin stars in Ireland—Patrick Guilbaud had two stars and Kevin Thornton had one—so to get one would really put us on the map. The thing about the Michelin system is that there are no rules you can look up to find out what you need to do to get a star, but as I'd worked in a three-star restaurant I knew exactly what the inspectors looked for.

Peacock Alley was awarded its first Michelin star in January 1998, a year and a bit after opening in South William Street. I was quietly pleased but being the kind of guy I am, I felt it was only the beginning.

Chapter 6
My worst mistake

IN 1998 LIFE WAS LOOKING GOOD. I had a Michelin star, I owned Peacock Alley and Lloyds, and they were both flying. I had a house in Rathfarnham with Domini and Lauren was thriving. Lots of offers were coming in for a third place and there was talk of an Asian concept. I was also doing consultancy work overseas, mainly in the Middle East, making quite a bit of money advising on start-ups, menus and staff training. At this stage I had all the trappings—a Rolex, a top of the range car that I'd paid for in cash, apartments with no morgages, and a lot of cash in the bank.

Being the sort of obsessive person I am though, that wasn't enough. I have to keep pushing myself, keep going for higher standards and bigger achievements all the time. I've always been a perfectionist. If I see a shirt hanging crooked in the wardrobe I can't rest till I've straightened it, if there are four bottles on a shelf, I'll have to take one off—the balance has to be right. Anything I do I always want to do to the highest level, and I'm never satisfied. Get one Michelin star? I want two. Open two restaurants? I want five. I always want to learn more, do more.

And the next step up was the second Michelin star. I felt Ireland had caught up with itself, there was lots of money around, people were eating out much more, they'd travelled and they knew what they wanted.

I also knew the star system. It's not just about craftsmanship and skills. It's about the environment and the trimmings—the carpets, linen, tables, chairs, the space between the tables and chairs, the drinks trolleys (how many different types of Armagnacs, Cognacs and Ports you have) the ratio of waiters to customers, your wine knowledge and product knowledge. The first star is mainly for the food. But the second is for food, service and a big upgrade on the environment, tables and settings. It has to be a good-looking restaurant. For the third star you need a view, a car park, maybe silk curtains and chandeliers, two staff to every customer, flowers changed after every service, 22 different types of bread coming out of the oven at 25 past 12 and on the table by half past, a pre-dessert, 12 petits fours, four of them hot, and the ingredients have to be the best of everything you can possibly find.

My big break?

I knew I couldn't get a second star in South William Street, the premises just weren't right. Then I got a call from the owners of the Fitzwilliam, a new hotel being built on Stephen's Green. I was ready to listen. One of them had been a customer in Peacock Alley and they wanted to know would I be interested in having a chat with them, as they were looking for someone to operate the food side—the restaurant, brasserie, banqueting, room service and bar food. So I met Michael Holland and Brendan Gilmore from Ampleforth, the company that owned the hotel. I later discovered that Michael Holland had a considerable reputation around town as an astute business man—someone described him as a black belt. They sold me this whole picture—the hotel's design was by Terence Conran, it was the best address in Ireland, there was a budget for this, a budget for that, a marketing plan, it was going to be great. They said they had great advance bookings, that I was the first one they'd talked to and I could move my little restaurant into their lavish hotel. Peacock Alley would be its fine dining restaurant, and Christopher's, the brasserie, would be less formal. The whole thing was really packaged and sold to me—my life of missed opportunities was over, I'd got the big break, the big one had just landed right into my lap. My hard work for years and years had paid off.

Under the licence I'd be paying Ampleforth a fee of £120,000 a year plus 6 per cent of my sales (net of VAT) plus a service charge and a portion of the rates and utilities. On top of that, of course, would be all my own costs—food, staff, laundry etc. for 120 covers (we had 80 in South William Street). My outgoings would shoot up but I was confident that so would my turnover and the profits would be there. Everyone close to me at the time and all my advisers were against it—my solicitor Lorraine Hayes, my accountant Brendan Malone, my uncle Frankie—they all said 'Conrad, don't do it'. I showed them the figures, I ran the numbers, what if this, what if that, and looked at three or four different scenarios.

For someone like me the glass is always half full, but for everybody else, especially the financial people, the worst case scenario wins. Domini and my brother both said the numbers didn't stack up, that there wasn't enough margin. But I asked myself how bad would it be if I had one restaurant that didn't make a lot of money, as long as we had the second Michelin star, we'd have the brand, we could open up a couple of bistros, brasseries, open a couple of cafés, get in the money that way. And then we'd have the beautiful restaurant upstairs in the Fitzwilliam, the fresh flowers every day—it'd be great. So I said 'The restaurant may not make us a ton of money but we'll make plenty of money on everything else so it'll be fine.'

Everybody said I was out of my mind but I did the best deal I could and at that stage, to make money or not, I wanted to be there. It was possibly the worst business deal of my life. It was to haunt me for the next ten years.

The worst possible start

I was told to be ready for the opening on 1 July so I decided to close Peacock Alley in South William Street in June, and spend that month preparing, training staff, writing menus etc. We'd got into the design stage— kitchens, fit-outs, crockery lists, cutlery lists, ice cream machines, vacuum pack machines, humidifiers—the best of everything. The hotel did the shell fit out, they paid for the kitchen equipment, and they were to pay for Peacock Alley's curtains, carpets, light fittings, tables and chairs. I paid for the Christopher's tables and chairs, the art, cutlery, custom-made china from Paris, the linen and the uniforms I also brought my wine cellar, and invested even more in it so as to make Peacock Alley's wine list one of the best in the country. We hired and trained 15 new staff so we now had 39 staff.

Closing down for a full month was a major mistake. Costs had gone through the roof but we had no turnover coming in. And two and a half weeks into that break we realised that there were huge delays with the building—it wasn't going to be finished on time. Rumours that the hotel would miss the summer rush started to go round. My requests to the management for information on advance bookings were declined.

All my stock had arrived—wine, uniforms, delph, cutlery and glassware—but my restaurant was still not ready. I was told not to worry, that the hotel would sue the construction company for the losses due to the delay. Then I was told that they were going to open the hotel without the main restaurant, there'd just be Christopher's,

and when the hotel was completed, all attention would go to finishing Peacock Alley. Next thing all the builders were taken out of the restaurants and told to concentrate on the bedrooms, the lobbies and the rest of the hotel to try and get them finished. So while the hotel was being completed in haste, the restaurants were still virtual building sites.

Christopher's had a terrible start. It was supposed to be ready when the hotel opened its doors but on the first day the floor still hadn't been laid. For weeks, customers had to sit in a dining room with drills and hammers banging and builders walking around in dirty boots. The builders decided to put rubber between the glass tiles of the gangplank into Christopher's. Thousands of little rubber balls, like rabbit droppings, ended up on the floor. They were sticky with adhesive so I had to clear the restaurant and get in a specialist contractor to remove them. Then the wine chiller froze overnight ruining over £1,200 worth of wine. At least twice or three times a week the extraction system would break down and smoke out the entire restaurant. Chefs were left to cook in temperatures of 120°.

It was like *Fawlty Towers*—nothing worked. I had to take my senior management out of Lloyds to try to resolve all the problems. One of the worst moments was when two lunchtime customers and a member of staff got stuck in the lift for almost forty-five minutes, with no air conditioning and no microphone to the reception. The lighting in the lift failed. One of the guests was claustrophobic. Eventually, someone found the key to ground the lifts in a builder's toolbox and the occupants were released.

Doing the room service turned out to be a nightmare. The hotel was beautifully designed but there were lots of teething problems, as there always are with new buildings. If guests in a fifth floor bedroom ordered breakfast in the morning, it took 8–10 minutes to bring the tray from the room service kitchen to the bedroom, which meant the food was cold by the time it arrived. We couldn't use hot plates as there was nowhere to put them in the rooms and bigger trays or trolleys would not fit through the bedroom doors, so two waiters had to carry two trays for two people. Therefore to do twenty room service orders, required seven, if not eight, staff. To serve a sandwich in the bar, the waiter had to run up four flights of stairs. And there was only one service lift so I was constantly trying to stop the cleaning company from putting trolleys in it while lunch and dinner were being served.

To top it all the air conditioning failed at *VIP Magazine*'s launch party. Michael Doherty and John Ryan had had the idea for an Irish version of *Hello!* magazine—the Celtic Tiger was really getting going—and I arranged for the launch to be held at the Fitzwilliam. It was one of the big social events of the year, with 200 guests. It was supposed to be in Peacock Alley but it was still being finished so it had to be in Christopher's. The room was packed, it was a hot summer night, all the elegant guests in their Armani and Gucci were expiring in the heat and started leaving in droves. It was so embarassing.

When we did finally open Restaurant Peacock Alley in October—and we opened with a bang—there was a huge amount of snagging left to do, so while customers were having lunch there'd be drilling upstairs. I had to keep calling up the manager's office and say 'Listen, we've got a problem—I've got a dozen customers sitting in the restaurant and they're threatening not to pay the bill because of the noise.' I had lost my independence.

Perhaps the worst thing was that the hotel had very few guests. So I now had staff operating seven days a week providing breakfast, lunch, dinner, 24-hour room service and bar food to a nearly empty hotel. Turnover was nowhere near enough to cover the staff costs (at that time there was a huge shortage of good staff in Dublin so you can imagine what we had to pay to hire them), food, rent and all the rest.

I lost a lot of my customers from South William Street because of the long closure—my old clientèle did not come with me. They were a fun crowd, they really enjoyed my food and they didn't mind spending on good wine. I like to please all my customers no matter what they spend—I love it when a couple come in to celebrate something special and they have a really nice time and they haven't spent that much. But we also needed big spenders. In the Fitzwilliam it'd be a Kir Royale, two glasses of white, two of red and that was it. It was costing me a fortune to staff room service, banqueting and the bar, but it was erratic—there were either too many staff or not enough.

I now had a business that was breaking even with every penny being used to pay the current costs. This was the first time I wasn't making big profits so I had trouble recovering from the loss made during the time we were closed. I couldn't make a dent in the historical costs, so they just sat there.

We fall out

My relationship with the owners soured very quickly. My first problem was the extended closing time. Then there was the shortage of guests so my turnover was way too low. The difference between me and them was that they were getting richer and richer—because they'd now built an asset in a rising property market and growing economy—but I was getting poorer. Within two or three months of opening it went to lawyers.

The general manager was a guy called John Kavanagh. I always liked him, we got on very well. A certain amount of things were handled at his level. But when it came to the financials or the legals or anything to do with the licence I dealt with Michael Holland. He was a man who was used to everybody saying 'yes' to him. You didn't argue with him. In those days I saw him as an enemy who'd sold me something that didn't work. He agreed to renegotiate certain things in the short term, but the long term for me was that I had a sick business that wasn't going to get any better. The only way I was going to make it work was if I cut my standards, reduced the level of service and got rid of my qualified staff. To make a profit in that setup I'd have to provide a lesser quality product and I wasn't prepared to do that.

The contract I had with Ampleforth, the owners' company, as you'd expect with these high-powered businessmen, was very long and detailed, full of standard clauses covering all sorts of 'what-ifs'—how the contract would be terminated if I became insolvent, if I was charged with a criminal offence, if I lost the liquor licence. I didn't pay a whole lot of attention to those clauses—as far as I was concerned, I was going to make this thing work.

Domini and I split up

I was working night and day, every hour that God gives, trying to make it work—which didn't help my relationship with Domini. We'd made a very stupid mistake when Lauren was a few months old of selling the house in Rathfarnham and buying a house out in Newcastle, in Co. Wicklow. It was too far from Dublin, so when the pressure came on me in the hotel, I ended up staying in Dublin a couple of nights a week. Domini had stayed working in the business for a while after Lauren was born. She was never a partner in the business, our finances were separate—she had no responsibility for any of the problems.

So Domini was at home, looking after Lauren and I was in the hotel most nights, and sometimes round the clock, trying to save my business. We started to drift apart. So we separated amicably.

Cashflow problems mount up

So here I was stuck with a sick business that was leaking cash. I brought in lawyer after lawyer to try and negotiate out of the deal. Michael Holland kept saying 'Your costs are too high', and I kept saying 'You need to reduce the licence fee. Why should I get rid of expert senior staff who are needed just to pay you?' We had top personnel providing top service, from the sommelier to the floor manager—why should I cut my staff to make him rich? Michael Holland wouldn't see the numbers, he wouldn't bend.

We had to lay off the staff we'd hired, which we hated doing, and of course it got negative press. They now had our training and our secrets—our recipes. By this time I was completely out of the kitchen—spending time watching money.

I sold the lease for South William Street, the old Peacock Alley, for £200,000. But it was delayed into 1999 because the landlord wouldn't give his consent to the sale, so we had to keep paying the rent there even though it was lying empty. By summer 1999 I needed a cash injection.

I agreed to sell Ampleforth the furniture I'd provided for Christopher's and some of the paintings that I'd brought to the hotel. A lot of them were by Felim Egan—he's from Strabane so he's from the same part of the country as myself. Some of these paintings were variations on a theme so at a quick glance they looked alike and people often mixed them up. I said I wouldn't sell them the three that were hanging in Christopher's—Felim had given them to me because I'd bought so much of his work.

This deal, done in a hurry because I was desperate for cash to pay staff, was to blow up in my face. The owners did up an agreement which included two lists, numbers 1–3, the three by Felim Egan which were in Christopher's, that I was keeping, and numbers 1–16, which were in Peacock Alley which I sold to them. Myself and Tom Mannix, Ampleforth's group financial director, signed a receipt for the 16 paintings for £20,000. It was dated 16 July 1999.

The cash flow problems didn't improve. I started going to 60 or 80 days with some suppliers, I had the fish man and the vegetable man coming to me but I wasn't able to pay them on time. I was battling to pay everybody but the cash flow just wasn't there. If your costs are higher than your income you can keep it going for 60 or 90 days but either your sales have to go up or your costs have to come down. I was doing everything to do both. But I wasn't prepared to cut my standards, I'd rather go bust or close.

So I said to myself 'I'm not working these hours, these days just to pay them and not to be able to pay anybody else. I'm going to reduce what I'm paying.' I said to the owners 'That's all I can afford to pay you, take or leave it' but they wouldn't hear of it, so the lawyers' letters kept coming. The more stressed I got, the more agitated and depressed I got and the more bitter towards the owners.

All the money I'd made over three or four years of trading brilliantly was just diminishing before me. I sold my apartments, I sold this, I sold that, but of course when you have to sell something in a hurry you have to sell it cheaper. And tourist numbers fell for a while because of foot and mouth disease and a few other things. There were definitely challenges for business. But I was still getting huge media, still keeping very high standards, and I kept my Michelin star.

At that stage not a lot of people would have known that I was having trouble making ends meet. The odd supplier was getting paid late but that was about it. But the cash flow problems got worse and worse.

I re-launched Christopher's and named it Mango Toast. It had an Asian theme, so it was completely redecorated with bright colours; the Felim Egan paintings didn't suit the new decor so I moved them to Peacock Alley. They were just leaning against a wall and I was afraid they'd get damaged so I brought them home for safekeeping. The cash flow problems continued. I was trying to keep all the balls in the air, getting involved in other deals to try to get money in, and all the time obsessing about the food being right, going mad because the chocolate fondants in Lloyds were cooked for six instead of six and a half minutes. Running one restaurant is hard enough but trying to run three at a high level requires huge management skills, and you can't really do that and be totally focused on the food as well.

Lloyds had been doing well, but I was personally consumed into the hotel, because it was all new and there was so much stuff happening so Lloyds got ignored a bit. Then I fell out with the landlord over rent and closed it. In the summer of 2000 I got into trouble with the High Court because I didn't go to a hearing about the rent dispute, my solicitor went instead. I was on anti-depressants by this stage, and I also had stomach ulcers.

In November 1999 after a year and a half of huge losses I did another deal with Ampleforth—I kept and ran Peacock Alley but no longer provided any of the other services. I said 'I'll pay you a fee plus a per cent of turnover but I'm not doing Mango Toast any more and I'm not doing the room service or any of the other stuff any more.' Ampleforth said they would back Peacock Alley but they wanted a share in it. At first, I said 'Why should you have a piece of my business? It's my business, I've built it up,' but I needed the support.

They guaranteed an overdraft facility of £50,000 with the Bank of Ireland and they got 25 per cent of the business. It was done through a company called Etonstar with a new agreement, with the same sort of conditions as the previous one. There were three directors—myself and Michael Holland and Tom Mannix of Ampleforth. After that all the Peacock Alley financial transactions went through the Etonstar joint bank account which required signatures from both them and me. The financial administration was done by the Ampleforth people.

Now I just had the restaurant in the hotel but the problem was I still had the old debts, so although Peacock Alley was flying, taking in £40,000, £50,000 a week, it was the same scenario, meeting high costs and trying to pay off old debts. Because of the cash flow problems I was selling various things to try to keep the show on the road. I had a house in Killiney, with a bedroom specially decorated for Lauren, but I couldn't keep up the mortgage payments and I put it up for sale. By now I was in *Stubb's Gazette*, there were judgements coming in against me from all directions, mainly from suppliers, and the landlord of Lloyds got a charge against the house. In November 2000 the High Court made an order that I was not to sell it.

The Revenue was owed VAT and PRSI, and they put an attachment order on the Etonstar account. I was so stressed by this stage that I couldn't sleep, I couldn't sit still, I was desperately trying to stave off bankruptcy. The medication I was on didn't help a whole lot—the Prozac had side effects that I hated. Looking back, I realise I was on the verge of a breakdown.

Towards the end of November I decided to raise a bit of cash on some things from my house. An auctioneer from Thomas Adams in Blackrock came out to the house, looked around and offered a £9,000 advance for some furniture and paintings, including my three Felim Egans. They accounted for about £3,000. The £9,000 was deposited immediately in the Etonstar company account which I jointly operated with the hotel owners. I had the option of buying the stuff back within a short period otherwise they would go to auction. It was basically a pawn arrangement.

Taste, taste, taste throughout the preparation

'You're under arrest'

On 7 December 2000 the police rang me and asked me to come in to Harcourt Terrace garda station. 'Why?' 'Ah sure, we just want you to come in about the paintings. There seems to be a discrepancy here. We want to you to sign a statement to say that you own them.' I got one of the staff to drive me round to the station and asked him to wait while I signed the form. I was rushing to get back to the restaurant—I was under huge pressure that day because my sous chef was off sick and I had a couple of high profile parties booked in for dinner that night.

When I went in they said 'You're under arrest', and took my phone and medication. They said 'Michael Holland has made a complaint about those paintings. What did you do with them?' I told them there was an agreement, that there was no discrepancy, but they didn't seem to be interested and put me in a holding cell. They left me there for an hour. I was going up the wall—the kitchen staff were waiting for me—I couldn't believe this was happening.

Then they took me out and interviewed me. Over and over again I told them to get the agreement, the paintings were mine, but it was no good. All I could think about was what was happening in the restaurant. I needed to be there, I thought of my guests turning up that evening and what sort of meal they'd get if I wasn't there to cook for them. The guards told me that they were extending my detention for another six hours. I could see that they weren't going to let me go if I didn't say anything, so eventually I said 'Yes, I stole the fucking paintings, now let me out.'

At that stage all I wanted was to get back to Peacock Alley and start cooking—I'd have told them my granny stole the paintings just to get out of there. So I signed the statement they had written. I thought the whole thing was ludicrous, I was sure that it would all be sorted out in the morning, when everybody spoke to each other, and the guards would realise then that it was all just a silly mix-up.

When my solicitor Gerald Kean was called he was round to the station within five minutes. The first thing he said to me was 'Don't say a word.' I said 'It's too late'.

By the time I got out that night, after 11 o'clock, there were dozens of photographers outside. Next day there were newspaper headlines 'CONRAD GALLAGHER ARRESTED OVER SALE OF PAINTINGS—QUESTIONED ABOUT ALLEGED THEFT'. And every single supplier and creditor was banging on my door.

Chapter 7
Every door closes

FROM THAT MINUTE ON, from the day I was arrested in December 2000, I was treated differently in Ireland. The velvet ropes weren't lifted any more. The invites to all the launch parties stopped arriving. The 'friends' stopped ringing and the customers stopped coming. Everything changed. I'd gone from being 'TOP CHEF' to 'CHEF ACCUSED OF ART THEFT'.

About ten days after my arrest, the two Ampleforth directors of Etonstar, Michael Holland and Tom Mannix, resigned as directors of Etonstar, and informed me that they had written to the Bank of Ireland cancelling their guarantee of my £50,000 overdraft facility. They also stated that Ampleforth would no longer be administering my accounts. I was glad to have them out of my life and to be back running my own business because they were always the first to be paid and I was the last.

Somehow I managed to keep the show on the road, paying staff, keeping the bank off my back, though it became harder and harder to get credit. I got really depressed—I might not be the greatest businessman in the world but I'm not a thief and it really hurt me that people were saying that I was.

The hotel wanted rid of me but I said 'This is my business. I'm not going anywhere.' Anyway I had nowhere to go. I carried on paying them. Although I was working away, paying my bills, keeping the wolf from the door, I wasn't making a lot of money for myself personally. A file had been sent to the DPP and as long as that hung over my head there were no endorsements, no writing articles and no TV work as all that side of the business had dried up. I'd had had a very lucrative business doing all of these things.

London lifeline

Early in 2001, the concert promoter Vince Power, of Mean Fiddler, threw me a lifeline and I grabbed it. We'd known each other for a while and had built up a sarcastic rapport. He was opening a 10,000-square foot restaurant in London in Shaftesbury Avenue in the theatre district and he wanted someone to front it. He made me an offer to go over and set it up for him, find the staff, write the menus, all the usual things.

I started going to the UK every week, earning a good fee from Mean Fiddler, and looking after Peacock Alley at the same time. So I was over and back, in and out of the Fitzwilliam Hotel and at that stage if I'd walked past the owners or the manager, I would have ignored them and they would have ignored me. And if there was a problem my lawyer called me. But I was in there, and I was staying.

London is hard to crack at the best of times and Irish food to most people meant bacon and cabbage—I had to work on changing that perception. I brought over great staff from Dublin and applied my Michelin star standards to the food, the décor, the lighting, the music.

I established the restaurant's main bar as a lounge by day where people could relax and have coffee, and then in the evening it turned into a trendy cocktail bar.

The restaurant was heavily dependent on theatre audiences and especially the two main musicals at either end of Shaftesbury Avenue, *Peggy Sue Got Married* and *Notre Dame de Paris*. It wasn't the best of locations and attracting the glitterati was uphill work. I hired the right PR company, and systematically partied in all the celebrity hotspots with the main—but not only—aim of making contacts.

In London, profile is everything. Vince, as a concert promoter wanted to fill venues, that was his business, so

Bill Clinton came to dinner with me in Shaftesbury Avenue—we were joined by Bono and Ronan Keating.

that was a big part of my role. I needed to attract rock stars and celebrities and I could do that. I was the chef for the MTV Awards in Frankfurt that year (I'd done it in Dublin before and was asked to do it again the following year in Barcelona) and it got fantastic media coverage which really helped bring people into the restaurant.

Conrad Gallagher Shaftesbury Avenue opened quietly in August with the big spectacular opening planned for September 2001—probably the worst timing possible as it turned out. Everything came together and we started getting reviewed in all the important papers. The reviews were mixed but on the whole they were positive. Slowly but surely the celebrities started coming through the door—first the IT girls Tamara Beckworth, Victoria Harvey and Tara Palmer Tompkinson, then Kylie Minogue, Sophie Ellis-Bextor, David and Victoria Beckham, Elton John, Madonna and Prince Andrew. Bono, Ronan and Yvonne Keating came from Ireland, and Bill and Chelsea Clinton celebrated a family occasion there. We hosted Robbie Williams' birthday party.

Then 9/11 happened. The Americans stopped coming, the two musicals closed, other theatres were shutting, the West End became a ghost town. Restaurants were in trouble—even The Ivy started to advertise. It was a difficult time.

And London proved too much for one of our team.

The saddest thing

One of the team who came over from Dublin was a really talented young chef. He'd been a protégé of mine ever since he turned up at Peacock Alley in South William

Street asking for a job. He looked so young I asked him how old he was. 'Nineteen,' he replied. 'No, you're not,' I said, 'you can't be more than fifteen.' So he admitted that was his age, but then he said 'Well, take me on anyway—you lied about your age when you got started.' So of course I couldn't resist and I trained him and he showed real skill and commitment.

London overwhelmed him and he took his own life in November 2001. He was only twenty-two. It was heartbreaking. I went back to Dublin to pay my last respects. The day after the funeral I was arrested and charged at Dublin District Court with larceny and obtaining money by false pretences. It was humiliating but the death put everything into perspective.

I fall out with Vince Power

With the lack of tourists, and the general downturn, turnover forecasts for Shaftsrbury Avenue had to be downgraded. The pressure came on us all, and instead of concentrating on the food and building up the business I found myself in an office again, going over figures and trying to cut costs. I was working seven days a week, flying back and forth between Dublin and London.

I'd been spending so much time in England building up my customer base there that, although the standards were as high as ever in Dublin, I started to lose some of my clientèle in Peacock Alley—customers liked to see me and I was there less often. The hotel owners definitely didn't want me there any more. I remember I came in one day and I was told that John Kavanagh had been showing Kevin Thornton and his wife around that morning.

Coming up to Christmas, things got really fraught between myself and Vince Power—we were fighting about everything—costs, standards, music. I really liked him, and he gave me a great opportunity in London but our relationship started breaking down because of the financial strains.

I was becoming more and more exhausted. I took a few days off over Christmas with my family and thought about my future. In the new year Vince Power and I decided to part company. To this day I regret that we fell out.

The end

After I parted company with Vince Power myself and Michael Holland had several conversations on the phone. There was no way I could keep Peacock Alley going without the Shaftesbury Avenue money coming in because a lot of the time I was using it to pay the bills in Dublin.

I had got an eviction notice at my house in Killiney. They gave me a month to get out and the sheriff was after me for money for taxes and this and that. I had no money, no deposit for an apartment and the likelihood was that no one would even rent me an apartment because it was in the paper every day that I was broke. The front page of the *Star* had the headline 'CONRAD TAKES THE BUS TO WORK', with a photograph of me getting off the bus. Every single week there was the most scathing stuff in the press, they would take something and blow it out of proportion. I was shocked at how quickly things turned against me. There were the most awful rumours going round. One was that I had only two months to live.

It all became too much. In the new year, I said to the hotel 'I'm throwing in the towel.' I told the staff and then it was all over. Everything was closed down.

Licking my wounds in New York

The trial wasn't going to happen for ages. In January 2002 the DPP offered to have the case heard in the District Court if I pleaded guilty to theft but I wasn't a thief so I refused. I was remanded on bail. Then in March it was decided I would be sent forward for trial in the Circuit Criminal Court, there'd be hearings that I'd have to attend then the trial date would be fixed. I packed up my house, sent a load of stuff to my parents' house and went off to the States with nothing. My brother was in New York and I knew that I had enough friends and contacts still there to keep me going.

The parasites would say to me 'You fled.' I didn't flee anywhere. I came back for hearings. What was I to do? Sit around and wait? I was ruined in Dublin. It was finished. What was I to stay for—to go and get a job in a café somewhere? The sheriffs of the court came, they took away my car, they threw me out of my house. There was nothing for me. There was nobody knocking on my door saying 'Do you want to come and work for me?' It was 'He's been accused of stealing paintings, he's gone bust, no one can touch him.' Every door closed for me; people stopped returning calls. I didn't run away from my debts, I didn't defraud people. My business, like lots of others, failed, and creditors lost out. I really regret that people lost money—it's really tough on them. But that's always a possibility in business—I know that through my own bitter experience of taking risks and losing money

So that was it. I went away off to New York and licked my wounds. I had three or four very dark months. I was due to go back to Dublin for a hearing in May, but I was too depressed to go. My psychiatrist sent a report in to the court and the hearing was adjourned for a couple of weeks. I went over to Dublin on 29 May and the trial date was fixed for 15 October. I was remanded on continuing bail and I returned immediately to New York.

Everything hit me at the same time and I had a kind of mini breakdown. The court case was hanging over my head, there was a huge amount of negative press every single day about me. Another lump appeared so I was having tests to see if the cancer had returned. The relationship with my family had started getting very strained, I hadn't seen Lauren for ages. I had no idea what my future held.

It was my intention to get a job, to work. I applied for certain jobs, went for interviews and I'd get on great, but then they'd do their searches and that was it. They'd Google me and all they'd see would be 'bust' and 'paintings', pages and pages of press coverage.

It seemed no-one would hire me as long as the painting thing hung over my head. I even considered changing my name at one stage.

On top of the world again

Somehow I got back up. I was sorting out my Green Card and seeing if I could get further rights and citizenship. I got in touch with people I knew in New York and rekindled a lot of old relationships. Any of my friends from the

States that came to Dublin used to eat at Peacock Alley and always had a good time, so there was a lot of goodwill out there towards me and people who wanted to help me get a leg up.

One day I was walking past a place in Manhattan, in Midtown, which was the new happening area in New York and I saw a 'To let' sign. I called the agent and asked to see it. It was an old cigar bar and it was perfect. It had a kitchen in the back and a nice big bar along one side. I decided to keep it low key. I met the landlord and said I wanted to create a little lounge bar, with cocktails and really nice tapas. I said I was a chef by trade but didn't want to cook at the moment, that I was more interested in having a night time business with a club aspect to it. I said I'd open at six in the evening and keep it going until four in the morning. He liked the sound of that, so we did a deal where I got a long rent-free period in exchange for doing a lot of work on it.

I was owed a bit here and a bit there, and a couple of friends put some money in, so between the jigs and the reels I managed to get the money together. A couple of old friends from New York helped out as well, and they agreed to defer payment. I begged and borrowed and by hook or by crook, I got the place open. I called it Traffic.

It was a really funky cocktail bar, with ice white windows, white banquettes inside, low tables with tiny candles, music playing all the time and beautiful cocktail waitresses. I'd play ambient music for the early part of the evening, then after ten thirty there'd be R&B or house music—different themes every night—and delicious Asian Fusion tapas—duck confit spring rolls, spicy prawn toast, selections of dim sung and sushi and lots of wok and noodle dishes. I concentrated on the managing and marketing, making sure the food and cocktails were right and the staff were on point.

I've had a lot of bad luck and a lot of good luck in my life and now my luck turned. Somebody from P. Diddy's organisation lived two doors up and used to walk past it on her way to work, so she could see it coming together every day. The night we opened she looked in and said 'This is marvellous'. She said 'I work for Bad Boy Records and we're having an event in two weeks' time and P. Diddy's coming. We'd love to hold it here'. So they did and then it was lift-off.

The *New York Post* ran an article on page 6 saying that Midtown was now the place to be and that a new bar called Traffic had received P. Diddy's seal of approval. My name was never mentioned and there was never an Irish element to it, but after that, every little groupie came by to see if they could meet P. Diddy. Alec Baldwin came in, and some Irish celebrities when they were in town, and so very quickly it became a really hot spot. And it was the first time in my life that I made a lot of money without working incredibly hard. I was always there, standing at the door making sure the mix of people was right—young stylish women, hip guys—it was very different to what I'd done before. But I used the same standards and the same quality, and applied the same ethos to the service, aesthetics, lighting and music. And it worked.

So after that grim time, when I'd watched my businesses fold, been arrested for theft and my name was dragged down, I was getting back on my feet again. I'd got a nice apartment by that stage, a bit of normal living, and I was getting back with my family. Lauren had come over and spent four or five weeks with me and my parents had come over to visit. Everything wasn't dark—all of a sudden there was a bit of light. It wasn't like a cancer ward every day, things were getting a bit better.

The case catches up with me

But the case was still hanging over me, like a black cloud. The trial date came closer. I didn't want to go because I was trying to sort out my papers. (I'd got married over there but it didn't work out and I got divorced.) And after the buzz of Traffic opening, I had a bit of a setback, when the reality of everything settled back in. I was really worried about my visa—at that stage I had formally applied for my Green Card, but there were lots of issues about going in and out of the country. So many things had gone wrong, there was so much stuff happening, that I was afraid to leave the States in case I didn't get back in. There was also the expense of flying over and back. So I talked to my lawyer in Dublin to see if the trial could be adjourned. It seemed to me that though it was put down for October for when the courts reopened after the summer, it wouldn't actually happen until February or March and I thought my lawyer could push it out until then.

I wanted to keep trading in Traffic until it was properly up and running and I had a couple of months under my belt. A few days before my case came up again, my solicitor tried to have it adjourned but the judge refused. 'Mr Gallagher has already received more than enough leeway in this matter . . . If he wants to treat the court with that kind of attitude so be it.' When I wasn't in court on the trial date, 15 October, the judge said 'Mr Gallagher is a celebrity chef. He knows the consequences. He thinks he's above the law.' Next thing my mother called me and told me there was a warrant out for my arrest.

I couldn't believe it. I'd just opened up my new business, it was flying. Then this thing erupted like a volcano. It was all over the papers and radio and TV in Ireland. The press started calling Traffic, there were photographers waiting outside to capture a picture of 'the fugitive chef'. This was my new title.

The mad thing about it all was that this would normally be a civil matter, because it was a dispute between two sets of people. I wasn't some terrorist or drug dealer. I really didn't think that they'd spend money and time coming out to get me. Plus there's a big difference between issuing a warrant for someone and actually going to get that person. Especially over three paintings that were worth just a few thousands.

Now, if I set foot in Ireland I'd be arrested and held until my trial came up. I was constantly on the phone to my solicitor. I said 'Here's the deal. I'm quite prepared to come back. You set up the trial for 1 June or whenever, and I'll come back and wait for two months or whatever it may be, but I'm not going to come back and wait for six months and lose my business.' I didn't want to go home, get arrested, be held in Mountjoy for a weekend and go through all that embarrassment again. He went back and forth to the DPP but they wouldn't even talk. All they said was: 'Come home and sit in jail. We won't give you bail and we'll take your passport off you. And if you don't come back we'll come and get you.' I said, 'Well, I'm not leaving here.'

The other problem was I didn't have the cash to fight the case. I couldn't risk going to court without good lawyers but they cost a fortune. I would also have to cover my costs while I was in Dublin, which could have been six or eight months. Traffic was doing really well and I was able to go back to anyone who had deferred payment and pay them, and I repaid my parents for some money they'd lent me and soon I had the place paid off and all the money that came in was mine. But I didn't have anything like enough saved to pay the lawyers. I needed some cashflow in so that I could go over and defend myself with some money in my pocket.

Then the Irish authorities issued an extradition warrant. I never believed they'd follow through on it. I hired a lawyer in New York and asked if I could be extradited and he said 'Absolutely not. They don't have the power. You've got rights.' And I was pushing all the time to get my Green Card so I'd have even more rights.

So I stayed in New York, working away with Traffic and saving as much as I could. And then the unthinkable happened.

Chapter 8
Prisoner No. 61685-053

It was a normal Thursday night.

I was inside Traffic's velvet ropes with my head doorman, Dax. We were arguing with a man dressed as a woman who was notorious in the bars of New York because once inside he would lift his skirt and prompt the guys to whistle. We had a few parties booked in so it was a full house. As usual I was constantly on the go between the kitchen, the barman and the queue, making sure everything was running smoothly. I stepped outside the ropes for a few minutes and looked up the street. Something didn't feel right—there were five bulky guys in dark blue bomber jackets striding down the street towards us. They didn't look like customers. It still didn't register when I saw two more coming from the other side, and not even when I looked across and saw two big black SUVs and trucks with flashing lights. All seven of them blatantly jumped the queue.

'Are you Conrad Gallagher?' one of them said to me.

'Who wants to know?'

'We're from the US Marshal's service. You're under arrest.'

'For what?'

'You're wanted out of Ireland on an extradition order. You're coming with us.'

Then they went for me, one on each arm, knees in the back of my legs which dropped me to the ground, then a knee in my spine. They twisted my arms behind my back, jabbed handcuffs onto my wrists, ripped the chain from my neck and the bracelets from my wrists, and went at my pockets and legs as if I had a bomb, all the time firing questions and orders:

'Are you carrying any weapons? Lay down, stay down. Do not move, sir. Sir, do not move.'

Then one of them shouted my rights at me. We've all seen it a thousand times on TV but here it was being barked at me on the streets of Manhattan outside my own bar, while my customers and Dax stared in astonishment.

'You have the right to remain silent. Anything you say can and will be used against you in a court of law. You have the right to speak to an attorney. If you cannot afford an attorney, one will be appointed to you. Do you understand these rights as they have been read to you?'

They dragged me up off the ground and I screamed at Dax to call my brother and tell him I had been arrested.

Then they threw me into the back of the SUV. It was like something you see on *Cops*—you'd swear they were coming to take a mass murderer away. I asked as calmly as I could where I was being taken. All they said was 'MDC', which of course meant nothing to me, but that was the end of the conversation.

I sat shell-shocked in the back of the van, my hands cuffed behind my back, staring through the grille at the road opening up in front of us, not knowing where or what was in store for me. The journey took about 30 minutes and all the time the two Marshals gossiped freely as if I wasn't there, one was talking about cheating on his girlfriend on his night off with some other girl. And there's me in the back, invisible, the poor guy who thought his life had just ended.

Inside MDC—the Metropolitan Detention Center or 'Club Fed' as the inmates called it—I was held in a pen with other new detainees, mostly Colombians, blacks, Mexicans and a couple of Arabs. I sat there for hours, my mind racing with panicky thoughts—are they going to lock me up? This has to be a mistake—where's my

'Club Fed', otherwise the Metropolitan Detention Centre, Brooklyn. Its two grey square blocks are in no-man's land, stuck beside a dirty-looking bay and lanes and lanes of freeway—ten floors of concrete that in the dark looked to me like Alcatraz

attorney? What's happening in Traffic? If I'm held in prison how can I keep Traffic going? What have I done, how did I let it get this far ... After five or six hours I was taken out, photographed and fingerprinted. And I was given my prison number: 61685-053. That's when it really hit me, that there was no escape, I was now a prisoner, and only a number—'I'm not supposed to be a human being in this place', I thought.

I was told I could make one telephone call, so I called my brother and told him what had happened (I was only allowed 30 seconds on the phone).

Then I was led into an area with three pens. In Pen 1 I was introduced to the ordeal of the strip search. I was lined up against the wall with another 11 inmates and 12 prison officers facing us. One on one. Then the instruction came.

'Remove all clothing. Throw the clothing three feet forward', as they each pulled on plastic gloves. As we stood there naked, they searched our clothes. Then came the body search with the command 'Lift your sack', to ensure nothing was secretly stowed—further indignity for me because of having only one testicle after the cancer.

'Raise your arms above your head.' A prison officer stepped forward and inspected my armpits, behind my ears and ran his fingers through my hair, shaking my head to see if any contraband fell out. I was told to open my mouth and he looked under my tongue and checked my gums. Then he told me to turn around and face the wall. I had to show the soles of my feet one by one. Then we were all told to squat down. Spreading the cheeks of my arse, armed with a long narrow object, he then checked to see if I had anything up my anus. I often wondered during the many strip searches I endured, if the prison officers got some kind of pleasure from it. Every time a prisoner had to go to court they were strip searched.

We were then moved into Pen 2 where we were given fresh clothes, known as court clothes, and told to get dressed. The clothing was colour coded—yellow was for the most dangerous inmates. I was put in white. Then it was back to Pen 1 where I waited for what seemed like hours.

At about 12.30 a.m. I was told to pick up a bed roll—a towel, cup, toothbrush, set of sheets and a thin white blanket—and brought in an elevator to the eighth floor, then walked along a long corridor. The noise was horrendous—banging on cell doors, shouting, screaming, crying. Then I was thrust into a cell and the door was closed and locked behind me with not a word said. It was completely concrete and freezing cold. There was a toilet and three bunk beds—the top bunk was empty, and there were two black guys snoring in the other two. I climbed up as quietly as I could—I was terrified of waking the other guys in case they'd attack me.

I was in shock. I couldn't believe I was in jail—over three paintings worth £3,000! I hardly slept at all that first night—I remember my mind going round and round in circles. Every couple of hours the peephole opened, somebody looked in and then closed it again.

At about four in the morning I was taken out of the cell and told I was going to court for a bail hearing. It was down to the pen again, but this time there were maybe 30 other inmates in there too. It was hot, sticky and very unpleasant. We were strip searched again—checked all over, bending over, being poked at and examined like animals. Then we were given back the clothes we'd been wearing when we were arrested and told to put them on for the court appearance. My black suit was creased and dirty from when the marshals jumped on me.

Next we were put into another pen where we were handcuffed, shackled and chained at the belly; then we were led in a line into a Bluebird prison van—they'd passed me in the street many times and I'd never wondered what it would be like to be inside one. Walking in file with the other prisoners, all I could do was take baby steps—the inmate shuffle—if I tried to walk faster my ankles would jar and I'd jolt the other shackled prisoners. I was afraid I'd trip the whole line up. I kept asking myself, 'Where did I go wrong?'

Sitting in the back of the van, on the way to Brooklyn Court, I hoped that somehow my brother had got my lawyer for me and that he'd arrange bail. At the courthouse they put us in a holding cell. There was a row of bench seating—but not nearly enough for all of us—an open toilet and a sink. It was now about 8.30 a.m. We lay around all morning waiting for our numbers to be called. There was never any mention of Conrad Gallagher in prison: I was known and addressed only as Prisoner 61685-053. The minutes that passed seemed like days. The only distraction was trying to avoid eye contact when an inmate positioned himself on the toilet to relieve himself.

Eventually, around 1 p.m. my number was called. I was brought to a small room and told my lawyer would be right in.

Instead of a top criminal lawyer with bail organised, in came a public defender. It turned out that my lawyer wanted $20,000 up front and there was no way I could come up with that kind of money.

'I'm your court-appointed attorney,' the public defender said. 'We have a few minutes before the judge calls us. So, what's the story?'

'I'm innocent,' I said. 'The paintings were mine, they'd no right to come in and pick me up off the street. Ireland has no jurisdiction in this country. I should be let out on bail, let's fight this.'

'I've read your case,' he said. 'You've no chance of bail.' He also said that I should give up my right to contest extradition.' Then he said, 'Hold on, I will be back in a minute Mr Gallagher,' really patronising—like a schoolteacher. But it wasn't a minute before he returned, it was maybe twenty, and all he said was 'OK, we're up.'

From the meeting room to the courtroom was about 100 feet. I had that length of time to tell him why the judge should grant me bail. I spluttered—I have cancer, I employ 30 people, I will put my business on bond, my friends will bail me out, I will go on house arrest. I stammered as fast as I could to tell him everything before we got to the courtroom. As we entered the courtroom I knew I was fucked. He said, 'No matter what, don't say a word.'

I listened to the prosecutor call out the charge: 'Stole three paintings from Fitzwilliam Hotel, Dublin, Ireland, worth £9,000. Sold them for £9,000'.

I said to my attorney, 'No, they were sold for £3,000.' The £9,000 I'd got wasn't just for the paintings, I'd sold other stuff with them. The attorney turned around and told me to shut up. My mouth dropped in horror. I wanted to dismiss him that very second and represent myself. He never mentioned anything about my business, my health, that I was in no way a flight risk. He said I had jumped bail to New York—but he didn't say that the Irish authorities knew where I was at all times and that I had gone to Ireland for court appearances. He told the judge his advice to me was to say nothing.

The judge looked down from his chair—he seemed surprised—and said 'Only in special circumstances is bail allowed in extradition cases. Does your client understand his rights?' I shook my head but the attorney replied, 'Yes'. He should have set out that I had ties in New York, that I was no risk, that I was happy to hand in my passport. But the judge wasn't having it because I had been out on bail in Ireland and I hadn't made the trial.

So that was that. I was told I would have the option of contesting extradition at another hearing. But in the meantime it was back to prison.

Chapter 9
A month in hell

Your role in preventing sexually abusive behavior
Here are some things you can do to protect yourself and others against sexually abusive behavior:

- Carry yourself in a confident manner at all times. Do not permit your emotions (fear/anxiety) to be obvious to others.
- Do not accept gifts or favors from others. Most gifts or favors come with strings attached to them.
- Do not accept an offer from another inmate to be your protector.
- Find a staff member with whom you feel comfortable discussing your fears and concerns.
- Be alert! Do not use contraband substances such as drugs or alcohol; these can weaken your ability to stay alert and make good judgments.
- Be direct and firm if others ask you to do something you don't want to do. Do not give mixed messages to other inmates regarding your wishes for sexual activity.
- Stay in well lit areas of the institution.
- Choose your associates wisely. Look for people who are involved in positive activities like educational programs, psychology groups, or religious services. Get involved in these activities yourself.
- Trust your instincts. If you sense that a situation may be dangerous, it probably is. If you fear for your safety, report your concerns to staff.

The pain of those first few days in prison was like nothing I had ever felt. The uncertainty was crippling. I had no idea what was going on outside, if Traffic was open, if creditors were banging on the doors, if anyone was fighting for it, for me, to get me out or if I was going to be stuck inside for who knew how long. I was petrified. I was afraid of losing the business I'd built up after everything had crashed in Ireland, of going back to those dark days, of the cancer coming back . . . I thought of Lauren and what she must be thinking. As soon as I could I asked the guards if I could use the phone but they said I would have to wait till Monday—three days. That seemed like an eternity. I didn't wash, I didn't eat, I couldn't sleep. It was a waking nightmare.

The only thing worse than the uncertainty was the fear. The atmosphere was violent and tense. I heard screaming and crying at night. I started imagining all kinds of visions of men being beaten and raped. I lived in terror of everything—I was just a chef but here I was locked up with murderers and rapists!—the other prisoners, the guards and of some horrible unknown shit happening to me out of the blue. And I had no protection. I was one of the few whites and I could feel the hatred. The blacks, Hispanics and other ethnic groups stuck together—but as an Irishman I had no one. I knew that even making eye contact could be a huge mistake. And there was no point looking to the guards for protection, they could be as dangerous as the prisoners. I was completely on my own.

And then it came. I tried to stay in my cell as much as I could those first few days but I couldn't avoid it any more. They told me I had to shower. Going in I heard this hissing sound. I couldn't make out what it was so I instinctively turned round. Then I realised it was other inmates hissing and pointing at me—'*culo mio*—your ass is mine'. I caught the eye of a huge black man openly masturbating and grinning at me. I'm a big guy but when you're up against mass murderers, drug barons, and psychotics you've got little chance of defending yourself. Someone grabbed my hair from behind—I used to wear it pretty long—and next thing I was on the floor taking thumps. I crawled back to my cell, bruised all over.

You can't tell anyone or say anything—that would be suicide. I had to take it on the chin.

I spent a long Sunday waiting. The sun was shining outside but each time I looked at it my stomach would go into shock as if I was going to faint or just break down. I had the worst visions in my head, everything was just upset.

Eventually Monday morning came. I still hadn't slept. I got up at 6 a.m. to use the phone but there was a ton of forms to be filled in and I was only granted a call at 12.30 p.m. I called my brother Keith. He was under huge pressure trying to deal with reporters. He had dropped everything for me and gone in to Traffic to try to keep it going. And he told me the papers were saying I'd go down for anything up to twenty years and that our parents were in a bad way. Everything I'd feared was happening.

Then my luck changed. When you're detained first you're basically quarantined, until they check you out for various diseases. They gave me a full medical with blood and psychological tests and then I was told that I was going to be moved—to the general section as it turned out. Nothing was explained, it was just more uncertainty. But it couldn't be worse than where I was, I thought. I had to get changed again, out of the orange jumpsuit into a cream uniform. A guard walked me down a long central passageway with a door at the end. When he opened the door the noise was just crazy—it was a huge room, the size of a sports hall crammed with inmates. In I went, with my mug, toothbrush, pillow and blanket. All the heads turned round to look at me. You could clearly see there were pockets of people, again they seemed to be segregated—Mexicans, Colombians, Hispanics, middle eastern, blacks and some white guys who I guessed were Italians. I felt the eyes of each group on me as I walked the long walk with my bedroll in my arms.

I made my bed and peeked out a few times to see what was going on, waiting to see who would speak to me or would they want to see what I was made of.

A huge black guy and a white guy turned up to the cell. They introduced themselves as Moses and Buppy and started asking me questions: 'How'ya doing? Where are you from? What are you here for?' I told them—and just hoped they'd believe me, that they wouldn't think I was some kind of informer.

Later I noticed two Italian guys sitting together. One was old and grey-haired and had a newspaper in his hands, and the other was middle-aged. I could see them looking at me and whispering together. They called Buppy over and started quizzing him, all the time looking straight at me. Then they signalled me to come over. I wasn't about to say no. They asked me some questions—'Are you Irish?', 'Why are you here?', and then one by one,

other Italian guys came from their cells—Charlie, Little
Dominic, Phil and John. They all gathered around me
asking questions in what seemed to be an interview, until
the old guy said 'He's good, he's with us'. His name was
Frankie and he was the head of the Italians in MDC.
He'd been sitting reading the *New York Times* as I was
being walked in. He showed me the paper. There was a
photo of me on page 7 with a full article: 'CELEBRATED
CHEF FACES EXTRADITION AND CHARGES'. It said I had
the option of an extradition hearing or waiving it and
returning to Ireland, that the art was worth $20,000. Now
the Italians knew I'd been telling the truth.

Frankie nodded his head and signalled for another guy
to come with him and me. I did what I was told and
followed him to his cell. I didn't know what to expect, but
he opened his locker and took out two candy bars, a jar
of peanut butter, a packet of Ritz crackers and a pack of
Marlboro Lights and said, 'Here you go son, you're Irish,
you're with us.' He looked at me as though to make sure I
understood. 'Anybody fucks with you, you tell them you're
with us. That's it.'

I sat down that night with my new-found friends and
amused them with stories about food and celebrities. Their
knowledge of food was on a par with my own. Especially
Frankie's. He was seventy-five years old but as bright as a
thirty-year old. He'd owned an Italian-style restaurant for
twenty years and when it came to classic Italian dishes he
had them down to a T. We talked for hours about food.

Over the next few days the Mafia guys all welcomed
me—they brought me in turn to their cells and gave
me food, underwear, socks, shaving cream, towels, extra

blankets and bars of soap. When they passed each other, they'd just nod their heads as if to say 'I see you, that's fine, I respect you, enough, goodbye'. I did the same. I was OK. I felt safe for the first time in days.

It turned out that my cell mate Buppy was half Italian and half Irish. He was a real gentleman. He was a neatness freak, so we got on well. He really watched out for me. He had fond memories of his Italian grandfather and it was funny how he explained things to me, schooling me on the ways of prison life. 'Stick with your own kind. White guys always shower and shave each morning. Never line up for seconds of food. Always make your bed in the morning. If you need anything, ask me or Charlie. Keep your mouth shut—they're all fucking rats in here.'

Frankie brought me to his cell one night. I had spent most of the day with him and I still didn't know why he was there and wasn't about to ask. He took a box from under his bed and opened it—it was full with a shower of print-outs from *Gang Land News*, a website about the Mob. As he showed me, I was half excited and half in shock as I realised that the man I'd just spent hours with was Frank ('Frankie Pearl') Frederico, a made man in the Luchese family, in prison on suspicion of double murder. There I was, sitting in the room of one of New York's famous mobsters. He'd gone on the run years before when the police asked him to submit hair and blood samples—DNA was going to incriminate him. He told me he'd hired OJ Simpson's chemist to fight the case. He'd been arrested just two months previously. He was carrying a money belt which the marshals apparently mistook for a bomb, so they jumped on his seventy-five-year old frame and removed it. All he was left with was a horrible memory and a ripped groin.

Another evening Frankie told me about two fig trees that his grandfather had brought from Italy. He had carried the seed and the soil all the way from the old country and planted them in their back garden. The police showed up one day with a digger and dug up the garden to see what they could find, so of course the fig trees were killed. He made several attempts to plant more fig trees with seeds and soil brought in specially from Italy, but they didn't take and the imported fig trees were gone forever. Telling this story made Frankie really sad, so we started writing some recipes. I knew talking about food would cheer him right up.

Being with the Italians put a little peace in my mind—you had to be in with some sort of crowd. The thing was always to stay around them. It was a way of being protected. So I ate lunch and dinner with them and played cards with them. We'd talk about all the things we'd cook when we got out—Frankie would describe veal cutlet with cèpes and madeira jus and I said what I wanted was a nice veal piccata with a side order of macaroni and glass of chianti—Frankie loved that.

The Mafia guys had serious power in MDC, they got away with a lot. At one stage they were bribing the guards to smuggle in food, marijuana, cosmetics—you name it. When I was in MDC there was a lot of bartering of food, mostly tins of mackerel, and cigarettes—that was the currency. The guards turned a blind eye, although of course things weren't done in plain view, we hid the fact we were doing it. The Jews and Moslems got different food from the rest of us, it was called common fare, the likes of raw vegetables, cans of tomato juice, and they had the use of a microwave, so the Italians bartered various things for that and I started cooking for them. I made stews and sauces—you'd be amazed what you can do with a microwave. I'd take the blade out of my razor and slice the vegetables, the broccoli, the onions, cauliflower, garlic, carrots, really fine. Sometimes we'd have stock cubes or spices and that would add a bit more flavour. We'd boil the pasta in the kettle. The slicing and the stirring and the tasting helped to pass the time as well as everything else. The Italians all had their suggestions and we spent hours talking about food.

My Italian friends carried on watching out for me but after a while the new white boy fanorama wore off. And in spite of their protection, all the time I was in prison I was afraid of being attacked and killed. There were vicious attacks there every single day. When you get a lot of men banged up together, most of them knowing that their lives are over, you can imagine what happens. Fights were constantly breaking out. The inmates were so strung out that any little thing would set them off and then the riot squad would charge in with their batons. We were given razors to shave with in the morning and guys would have them in the showers—they'd dance around you, waving them—they'd cut you up as soon as look at you. On top of that I was very depressed and stressed, my body was very stressed, I didn't know what was going to happen and there was no information on what the next move would be.

The routine was deadly monotonous, which was

torture in itself. At 6 a.m. every morning the cell door opened automatically. Very quietly so as not to disturb my cellmates, I would go upstairs to the communal area. It had concrete floors and blue painted walls. The tables and chairs were all metal and fixed to the floor. The guard would be sitting up on a big pedestal chair, and I'd join the line of inmates in our uniforms and slippers, queuing for breakfast. This consisted of a carton of milk and a slice of stale sponge cake. Then there'd be hours of hanging around until we all were locked into our cells again.

Then at 12.30 there'd be a scream of 'Chow!' The cell doors would open and everybody would run as fast as they could to get into the queue, grab a tray and line up for food. Lunch was Jello, two slices of bread, rice most days and then some unknown meat, fish or something else that I think even the best of food scientists would have trouble identifying. I asked the cook one day what type of fish it was and he said 'Sewerfish'. That made everybody laugh. Just looking at his greasy hair, dirty fingernails and rotten teeth would put you off eating. When they realised I wasn't going to eat it—it was like dog food—the other inmates started grabbing it off my tray. After that, there was more hanging around until we were locked into our cells again, then out for dinner which was just as disgusting as lunch. Then there was more hanging around and it was back to our cells for the night.

To pass the time I got into the habit of working out with Moses and some of the black guys. The routine took two hours each evening. Five of us in total—with me the only white guy. We used a table as a bench press, the staircase to do pull-ups and sit-ups with somebody sitting on your feet and then we used a black bin liner filled with water as a punch bag. We did sets of twenty of each so I had no trouble sleeping those nights.

I barely ate the whole time I was there. I studied myself in the mirror one day and I have to say I don't think I ever looked worse; you would be surprised what sixteen days in prison can do to you. Sleeping was difficult; I'd doze off for a while but then the nightmares would start. I missed my life. I thought of Lauren and what she must be thinking . . . One of the coldest, longest nights I have ever experienced was when the air conditioning in the cell was turned on full. I had all my clothes on plus two blankets, but it was no good. I was freezing. To make it worse, Buppy had a bad cold and chest infection so with the cold and him coughing all night, I spent the ten hours looking at the four walls wondering had I had all my punishment yet.

I got to speak to my parents at last and tried to reassure them that I was OK. How much longer would I have to put in—another week, month, how long?

Going to court for extradition hearings broke up the routine. It was the same story every time, up at four in the morning, in and out of the pens, strip search, into another uniform, into the chains, handcuffs, shackles around the ankles—basically being treated like a wild animal.

On the way down to change into court clothes for my first hearing I met Frankie. I was happy to see him as it meant I would have some company for the day, but he wasn't too talkative as he didn't know why he was going to court. He thought maybe it was because he was up on a new charge or because he was due to have a hernia

CONRAD GALLAGHER

operation. There was me and Frankie and about twenty other guys in the truck, some of New York's most hardened criminals, with armed guards all around us. Two of the prisoners were up for multiple murder. One of them was Peter Gotti—John Gotti's uncle.

Of course the bus had 'Prison' on it and as we went through all these neighbourhoods in Brooklyn, typical residential areas, the little children going to school would wave in the window—I asked myself did they think we were all murderers, rapists or bank robbers?

As before, we sat chained up for hours in the basement of Brooklyn Court, watching guys walking up and taking dumps in front of us in an open toilet. It was horrible, just horrible.

Eventually my number was called for my turn in front of the judge, and when they removed my shackles I politely said to the marshal 'Thank you, that feels better' and he responded 'Don't thank me, thank the American government'.

I'd decided not to fight the extradition. The problem was every time I talked to a lawyer about taking on my case they asked for $20,000 up front, and if I'd agreed all my savings would have been gone, so I made up my mind to just to sit it out and keep my money for when I got back to Ireland.

This time the judge was a lady and she seemed quite concerned about my welfare because I had cancer, so I regretted not putting in another bail application. When we got back to MDC we were all on lockdown, my first one; there had been a fight, so it was straight to the cell with no food or water until 6 a.m. The demons started again: what if this happens, what if that happens . . .

Some of the other prisoners told me that agreeing to return to Ireland was a mistake, as I'd never get back into the States again. So I decided to appeal the extradition after all and went to court again. It turned out I'd got bad advice—there'd be no problem if I was acquitted and even if I was found guilty I could appeal to the authorities to return. So I dropped the appeal. Then I was warned to be ready to move again. I was woken up in the middle of the night and taken to a holding cell. I didn't know what was happening or where I was being taken next.

It's over

In the morning the door opened and I could see two Irish guards standing outside, a man and a woman. I'll never forget the smiles on their faces. It was the two detectives who had questioned me that day in Harcourt Terrace, grinning from ear to ear and holding armfuls of shopping bags. They'd had to wait an extra day because of my extradition appeal so they'd had time to go to Macy's, Barneys and Gap. The male detective shouted at me 'I told you we'd get ye!' Then he showed me the front page of a newspaper over his shoulder. It had a photo of me and the headline: 'CUFF LUCK: COPS SCUPPERED IN BID TO BRING CHEF CONRAD BACK'. It was just a taste of what was to come.

Chapter 10
Limbo

I WAS PUT INTO A TRUCK with four or five guys with guns and driven to the airport. They walked me through JFK in chains and then put me in the back of an Aer Lingus plane, which was full of Irish people. The marshals wouldn't let go of me until I was physically on board the aircraft. They took the shackles off me, the Irish cops signed the handover papers and then handcuffed me—as if I was going to jump out of the plane! I had to sit with them, in handcuffs, for the whole flight while the Irish passengers ran down and took photographs of me with their phone cameras.

We landed at six in the morning and the two detectives arrested me as soon as I stepped off the plane. They walked me through Dublin Airport in handcuffs into the back of a police car, and then I was taken to Bridewell garda station. On my way to JFK I'd been allowed to call a solicitor, so I thought of my friend Carl Haughton. We'd known each other for years—he'd represented me in a few different things and we used to go for a few pints. I knew I could trust him, that he'd put his back into it. I didn't want to get some criminal lawyer that I didn't know. He came in to see me and got the ball rolling.

I was taken in a squad car from the Bridewell to the Four Courts—a distance of about 100 yards. As soon as the car stopped it was surrounded by photographers, cameras popping and reporters shouting questions and thrusting microphones at me.

I was brought into Court No. 26, still in the prison uniform. I was utterly exhausted—I'd been up since 4 a.m. the day before and I hadn't even been able to wash. The courtroom was jammed since there was a long list of cases to be heard that morning. But when my name was called utter silence fell.

Carl did his best for me—he apologised on my behalf for not returning for the trial in October and said it was because I was afraid it would get in the way of my application for US citizenship and would jeopardise my livelihood. He asked that I be granted bail but the judge said no and I was sent to Cloverhill prison in Clondalkin, where I was signed in with all that entailed—the searches, putting on the uniform, going through the whole bloody process again.

Carl engaged a junior counsel—Deirdre Hughes from Newry—and they went to the High Court that afternoon and I was granted bail on condition I put up bail money of £30,000, which I didn't have, and surrendered my passport, which was still in the States.

So I stayed in prison. Cloverhill was a pretty decent place—it was clean, the food was good. The staff were very firm and strict but they were fair—you couldn't go away disliking any of them. At that stage I hadn't eaten properly for six weeks so I'd lost a huge amount of weight. In the Brooklyn prison I'd put the food to my mouth alright, but it tasted dreadful, and even when it did taste OK I just didn't seem able to swallow it. I hadn't had medication in five or six days, I was completely humiliated and my body was totally stressed out. But the officers didn't take advantage, they'd let me take my food back to the room when I was feeling really down and stay there, rather than go out to the yard, which was usually compulsory. They would do what they could to make prison more bearable though nothing could take away from being locked up for twelve hours every day.

Sister B. was the prison nun. She was my greatest ally. She would make phone calls for me—we were allowed only one six-minute phone call a day—and she'd slip messages under my door and she kept me in cigarettes. I needed to get my bail sorted and my defence case going so those phone calls were vital.

The other inmates were quite friendly. Most of them were on remand waiting for their cases to come up. The Suitcase Murderer was in the cell next to mine. He was a Russian immigrant who killed a man who tried to chat up his girlfriend in a bar. After stabbing him 38 times, he decided to dispose of his body by cutting it up, putting the pieces in a few old suitcases and dumping them into the canal at the Portobello Bridge. The case was all over the papers. I used to see him in the yard and he'd say to me in broken English 'Hey, I saw you in the paper,' and then he'd ask me for a cigarette.

Some of the other inmates were heroin addicts who had turned to petty crime; and there was a homeless drunk who just needed a place to stay; there was a Dutch lorry driver who was in for drug trafficking, and a Canadian who was fighting extradition for a massive credit card fraud charge and then there were a few old ordinary decent criminals who had just got caught.

Breakfast was at 8.30 a.m.—tea, sugar, milk, cereal, and barm brack—this was the only time milk and sugar were given out. Then back to the cell. At 9 a.m. there'd be a rap at the solid cast iron door, and I'd be given a razor—it would be collected at 9.15. At 9.30 the cell doors opened. Then I had to make the bed, mop and brush the floor, and take a shower in the communal showers with 10-12 other inmates. Then it was out to the yard. This was an open area the size of a football field, surrounded by a wire fence and closely watched by the prison guards. I'd smoke, walk around and chat, read the paper, look out through the wire that fenced us in and wonder when the fuck I'd be getting out.

I didn't ask to see a doctor even though I needed my medication. The problem was that every single thing I said or did at that time ended up in the papers. So I was smart enough not to give anything away. A couple of friends came to visit me, and my father came. He had aged about twenty years.

Out at last

It took about six days to raise the bail money of £30,000—Carl got on to that—and get my passport Fed Exed over from the States. Carl arrived to pick me up with a grin on his face. His first words were: 'That was hard! Everyone wanted to bail you out until I asked them for the money and then they mysteriously didn't answer their phones.' But my old reliables came through as they always do. Carl handed me his phone and said 'Help yourself'. What a luxury—unlimited use of a phone! I called my parents, then Lauren as we drove in the rain and traffic all the way to Dublin.

Getting out of prison I had to give an address where I'd be staying and the only place I could think of was a Cellular Connections shop in Ballsbridge that my friend Colin Hayes owned. I had got to know him when he came in to the restaurant for dinner one evening, in the early days in Baggot Street, with Jonathan Philbin Bowman. God rest his soul, Jonathan, but I think he may have had one or two drinks too many, and he may have said something to me. I must have been a bit hyper at the time. I think he said the petits fours were too sweet. So I ripped the bill up, chucked the pieces in his face and threw the two of them out. A couple of days later I was standing in the restaurant and Colin appeared with another guy.

'Why are you here?' I said to him.

'I love the food' he said. 'And I did nothing, I didn't say anything to you.'

We both started laughing.

'What do you do?' I said.

'I'm in mobile phones. Do you have one?'

'No, why would I have a mobile phone? I'm here all the time.'

The next day he brought me a phone and that was it, we became great friends and we've stayed close all the way through. He's had plenty of ups and downs in business himself, so he understood, and we had a lot in common—we both had speed boats out in Dún Laoghaire at one time, we liked the finer things in life. We were both young entrepreneurs, willing to take chances. Porsche one day, bus the next. You're lucky with some, unlucky with others, you get up in the morning and just keep going.

I called Colin as we drove in to Dublin and he picked me up in town and rushed me off to Dalkey for my first shower and shave in freedom for at least six weeks. I changed into jeans and a T-shirt. Colin's wife Jenny cooked her roast chicken and spuds and Colin and I went for a few pints of Guinness.

The following morning at 9 a.m., my good friend Paul McMahon picked me up and drove me to Donnybrook Garda Station where I had to sign in twice a day until the trial started. And of course the photographers were waiting—in the paper next day there was a photograph of me getting out of the car and the headline. 'BAIL VISIT: CONRAD GALLAGHER, SPORTING A NEW HAIRCUT, ARRIVES AT DONNYBROOK GARDA STATION IN A FRIEND'S PORSCHE TO SIGN ON AS PART OF HIS BAIL CONDITION'.

I needed to get my hands on some money quickly. I had no clothes, no razor, not a penny in my pocket, no credit card or debit card, nothing—I had been ripped from my life. I started thinking how I could make some money. And of course everyone wanted an interview. So I said to myself, if they want me to fill column inches I'm going to do it on my own terms. *Ireland on Sunday* called me up. They wanted the juice of the prison. I said 'You want an interview? I won't do one, I'll do three and I want £30,000.' They agreed.

So on their front page on 25 May there was a huge headline 'MY RAZOR TERROR IN SHOWERS BY CONRAD GALLAGHER' and there were two more pages inside of an interview I did with them. It was all over the *Sunday Mirror* on the same date too, 'CONRAD—MY JAIL TERROR' but this time they were quoting 'friends'. And of course there were loads of photographs of me at different periods of my life, with different lengths of hair, clean shaven or with designer stubble—standing over a stove wearing my whites, in handcuffs in my court uniform, looking thoughtful in a suit, with a good-looking girl at Traffic.

Traffic was in trouble. The arrest had been all over the papers in New York, all over everywhere. But a couple of people I knew were interested in taking it over. I did a shotgun deal—I gave them two months to get a liquor licence, which would take my name off it, and they had to change the bar's name. I didn't want people trading on the name, Traffic, in case I wanted to go back and open up another one. I got a certain amount of money for it and called it a day.

Carl put in an application saying I wasn't going to be living at the shop, that I'd be living somewhere else and eventually, between Traffic and the jigs and the reels, I was able to rent a place and pay everybody back the bail money. I was able to see Lauren. I got phone calls and letters of support from friends and people I hadn't seen for a long time. A good friend Owen had not only lent me money towards the bail but he also provided me with an excellent BMW which was a lifesaver.

Preparing the case

We'd already started preparing the defence case. There were only a few weeks to the trial so it was very short notice for everybody. I asked Paul Mac to help me. He's a meticulous detail guy. He has a masters in mathematics and worked as a stockbroker for years and as a derivatives trader in Japan. He knows contract law inside out.

It was going to be a very high-profile case and we needed a top legal team. Deirdre Hughes was already on board. We got on really well. Both being from the North we have the same sense of humour and can't stand bullshit. She's a fighter—that's what I needed. Now we had to find a senior counsel.

The first few senior counsel Carl approached couldn't take it on. The only one I knew was Richard Kean, brother of my solicitor, Gerald Kean, who had a list of celebrity clients. I had met Richard at a party Gerald gave for his wife Clodagh's birthday—it was in a private castle in Switzerland. There were a hundred guests for the weekend, including Duran Duran, Ronan Keating, Paul Young, Finbar Furey and they all performed for us. The champagne flowed, we ate a fantastic buffet—it was great. Richard came across to me as being very posh, very funny and witty. He had a reputation for being a bull dog in court, and a bull dog with humour as well as being great with juries—he was exactly the person we needed.

Richard Kean

But when I called Richard he said, 'Conrad, I can't do it—I'm about to go out the door to go to Kinsale with the wife and kids. It's my first holiday this year, and I'm going to be gone for three weeks. There's just not enough time.' But then, as he was saying that he said 'Come out and see me anyway—I'll make a couple of calls for you.' Paul Mac and I jumped in the car and drove out to Richard's mansion in Killiney. It was just around the corner from my old house that I had lost the previous year. There it stood, unoccupied, very shabby, the garden overgrown, with a 'For Sale' sign outside. Richard was very straight, he just said, 'Tell me the facts, Conrad.' So I told him about the agreement I had with Ampleforth about the 16 paintings I'd sold to them and I told him what had happened. It was clear in my mind that, as far as the trial was concerned, there were two issues at stake. First, the contract clearly stated that I had sold them 16 paintings—the three paintings I was accused of stealing were not part of the sale to Ampleforth. Second, I had not personally benefitted from the sale of these paintings to Adams as the money had been deposited in the Etonstar joint account. We started going through the documents.

In their initial statements to the gardaí the Ampleforth people, Michael Holland, Tom Mannix, John Kavanagh and Stephen Carroll, said that I had sold them 16 paintings. However, they later changed their evidence, saying that they had made a mistake and that I had sold them 19 paintings.

I showed Richard the document I'd signed, confirming receipt of the £20,000, for 16 paintings. Then Richard said, 'Conrad, this agreement clearly states which pictures are yours and which are theirs. The ones on the list numbered 1 to 3, the ones which were hanging in Christopher's, are yours, and the ones on the other list numbered 1 to 16, hanging in Peacock Alley, are theirs.'

By now, we were starting to feel confident. 'After all,' we kept saying, '16 doesn't equal 19.' We took a coffee break and Richard and I went into the kitchen to make it. There was a plaque on the wall 'ANY BITCH CAN COOK'. We both burst out laughing. Then Richard went off to talk to his wife. He came back a few minutes later.

'Conrad,' he said, 'I'll do it. I'll take on your case.'

'But what about your holiday? Your family?'

'They'll go on down to Kinsale, I'll follow them later, and then I'll come back next week.'

It was fantastic—now I had a really good team. Richard asked Carl to get everything together for him so that when he returned from his few days' holiday he could put the case together. So over the next few weeks we went on the journey of preparing for the trial. It was very important that we spend a certain number of hours every day going through the facts of the case and getting all the information into a few pages, not fifty, so that when Richard stood up in court, he would have it at his fingertips. We knew we had to close up any gaps, so Paul prepared all the documents, photocopies and backup papers, going through it in minute detail.

We asked Frank Murphy, an expert in contracts, to look at the agreement. When he came back with his opinion he said that the way he read it the paintings were definitely mine.

'No matter how you chop it up,' Richard said, 'whatever was said or not said, maybe there was a misunderstanding, but the law is based on the contract, and it says they're your paintings.'

My biggest worry now was that all the press coverage seemed to find me guilty. I'd been in the papers so many times, called the 'fugitive chef', the 'celebrity chef accused of theft' etc. But pretty quickly the whole story came together. The contract to do the food in a five-star hotel under impossible conditions, the hotel opening with just one floor ready, the rest of the hotel being under construction, my business suffering and the relationship between me and the hotel souring as a result. We knew Holland's team's case would be that I was a bad licensee, that I couldn't pay my way and practically went bust in the hotel, so I took paintings that weren't mine and sold them. But, we had the agreement.

When we had prepared the best case we could and most of our subpoenas had been served, we found that my bank manager—a crucial witness for my defence—was away. The hotel owners had told the police that a suspicious lodgement had been deposited to an account—the Etonstar account—controlled by me. They did not tell the gardaí that it was in fact a joint account and that I couldn't withdraw money from it unless they had co-signed first. I needed the bank manager to tell this to the jury. I had deposited the money to relieve an attachment order the Revenue had made on it for unpaid taxes.

The weeks leading up to the trial were very difficult. And there was huge media interest. Every time I went anywhere there were cameras snapping and there were more photos and hostile headlines, 'RICH FRIEND WHISKS CHEF ROUND TOWN'.

All the waiting was dead time really, waking up in the morning, going for a run, signing on at the garda station, putting in the time. I wrote a good part of this book in those weeks so I supose it wasn't a total waste of time. While I was waiting for the trial if I walked into a restaurant three people would get up and leave. One of the most hurtful times was going into Roly's Bistro one night with a couple of friends. The chef, Colin O'Daly, was a good friend of mine. As I was sitting down I could hear this guy at another table telling whoever he was with all about me. He said it so loudly that we could hear exactly what he was saying. I was so embarrassed. Another diner got up out of his seat, spluttering with anger at the guy. It was a really horrible time.

Chapter 11
Thank God for juries

THE TRIAL BEGAN IN THE FOUR COURTS on 1 July 2003 in Court 29 of the Dublin Circuit Criminal Court. It was a bit of a circus in a way. Some of my friends were models and would turn up every morning to support me. The media had fun trying to identify all these gorgeous six foot-two women walking in—it was like a fashion show. The court was packed every day—with the legal teams, the witnesses, the media, onlookers from other courts, the public, my family and friends. I was put sitting in a kind of box, facing the jury—six men and six women. The judge was Yvonne Murphy. I was really nervous.

The charges were:

1) Stealing three abstract paintings by Felim Egan from the Fitzwilliam Hotel on St Stephen's Green on dates unknown between 2 and 22 November 2000.

2) Obtaining money by false pretences on 21 November in my home in Killiney with

3) Intent to defraud, by falsely pretending that the paintings were mine to sell.

I pleaded not guilty to all three charges.

The days in the courtroom were long and painful. As I sat and listened to all the evidence that was brought against me, watching Michael Holland in the witness box, as polished as ever, keeping his cool under Richard's cross examination, my confidence dropped. It was horrible to hear myself described as naïve, volatile, a bad businessman.

The prosecution started out as we expected, presenting me as practically bankrupt before I ever went near the Fitzwilliam. Michael Holland said that I was insolvent when I moved from South William Street. So that was all over the papers the next day 'Chef insolvent' and every day after that the most hurtful pieces of evidence would be headlines.

Hazel Hurley, my head book-keeper at the old Peacock Alley in South William Street, gave evidence that business was booming before we moved to Stephen's Green. 'It was a machine that worked,' she said. 'He ran the ship well. He was making money—I saw what was in the bank—and all his staff were very well paid right down to the kitchen porters. . . . but his expenses went through the roof when he moved to the Fitzwilliam. He should have changed his attitude to business affairs when he moved but he didn't.' That was true, of course, but I wasn't very happy to hear it said.

My PA at the Fitzwilliam, Sophie Flynn Rogers, described how being arrested and accused of stealing had devastated me. 'He told me "Sophie, they can call me many things, but I am not a thief"'. She said that when she was working for me at the Fitzwilliam I was always stressed and under huge financial pressure.

Then Richard got stuck in to Michael Holland. He has a marvellous booming voice and it was really dramatic when he cross-examined witnesses. He said I'd been duped and manipulated by the hotel owners.

They wanted me in their hotel because I was the premier chef in Ireland at the time. They'd promised 70 per cent occupancy rates and when that didn't happen my business suffered disastrously. He said I was a master in the kitchen, more comfortable with pots and pans than business plans, whereas Michael Holland was a director of 49 companies and he had a 'casserole of characters' to advise him, teams of accountants and lawyers.

Michael Holland said that he'd waived rent for a period and arranged an overdraft facility. Richard boomed at him that he was presenting the impression that he had acted kindly towards me, whereas the truth was that he had it in for me when he contacted the gardaí. 'The fact was the company wanted an excuse to get rid of Conrad Gallagher.' If my contract with the hotel was ended they would have had to give me compensation of £50,000—unless I was charged with an indictable offence. Michael Holland denied that he contacted the gardaí because he wanted to get rid of me from the hotel.

Frank Murphy, the expert on contracts, gave evidence on the second last day of the trial. He said that he would have told the hotel owners that they did not own the three paintings and that I did. The receipt for the £20,000 for the paintings was very clear that it was for the paintings listed 1–16 on the schedule and did not include another group listed 1–3, the ones I was accused of stealing. He said that the sales contract drawn up by the hotel for the paintings was untidily drafted and more care should have been taken with it.

Richard pointed out that in the sale contract, and in his original statement to the gardaí, Michael Holland referred to 16, not 19 paintings.

'As everybody knows,' said Richard, '16 always means 16, not 19.'

Closing statements were made on the morning of Tuesday 8 July, the sixth day of the trial. I didn't feel the day had gone well. The judge gave her direction just before lunch and I felt that it wasn't favourable to me. I got the

I CONRAD GALLAGHER of Peacock Alley care of The Fitzwilliam Hotel, Dublin 2, hereby acknowledge receipt of a cheque in the sum of £20,000 from Ampleforth Limited in respect of the purchase by Ampleforth from me of the following paintings numbered 1 to 16 on the attached list.

I further confirm that these paintings are owned by me personally and that there is no lien or debt owing to anybody or any company whatsoever in respect of the above paintings.

I further acknowledge that Ampleforth Limited are at liberty to take possession of the above paintings from Peacock Alley at any stage.

I also acknowledge that the fact that while paintings may remain on the walls in Peacock Alley, that I will at no stage have any claim lien or hold over the paintings and that I am only holding them on Ampleforths behalf with no claim to them.

Dated this the 16th day of July 1999.

Signed CONRAD GALLAGHER

Tom Mannix
GROUP FINANCIAL DIRECTOR
AMPLEFORTH LIMITED

The crucial document. As my barrister Richard Kean put it: '16 means 16, not 19.'

impression she didn't like me, that she thought I was an arrogant so-and-so and should get what I deserved. I was afraid that's what the jury would think too.

I'd been told to be prepared to be returned to prison. My legal team warned me that if I was found guilty I could do six months. That scared me.

Judge Murphy directed the jury. She told them to disregard what the expert witness Frank Murphy had said about the contract, because this was a legal matter and she, being the judge, was the only expert on law that the jury should consider. She also told the jury that it was important that they study the contract carefully and come to their own conclusions. She said jurors had to decide if I had acted fraudulently or whether I honestly believed that I owned the paintings and acted consistently with such a belief.

Then the court cleared for lunch. Every day so far I'd gone out to lunch with my legal team but that day the officers of the court stopped me leaving the courthouse— 'Sir, you can't go out to lunch today. You can't leave the building today.' Every other day of the trial the Fitzwilliam side had five or six people in the courtroom watching and listening and taking notes but they weren't there that day—and that worried me as well. I began to think they knew something I didn't.

The courthouse was absolutely packed waiting for the jury to come back with their verdict. After just two hours they returned. When they filed in, my heart sank. Not one of the six men and six women looked at me. I'd always heard that was a bad sign. Juries don't want to catch the eye of the poor guy they are about to send to jail.

I stood up and waited while the foreman read out the verdict. It was unanimous.

Theft—not guilty.

Intent to defraud—not guilty.

Obtaining money by false pretences—not guilty.

Judge Murphy said I was free to go.

It took a few moments to sink in.

Tears ran down my face—I was free! We all hugged and clapped—even Paul Mac had tears in his eyes. As I hugged my legal team, friends and family crowded round, congratulating me and my phone started to ring.

We made our way outside through the crowd, to popping cameras and shouted questions. The taxi drivers were beeping and cheering as they drove past. Construction workers on a building site nearby cheered. It was comical. There was a short press conference. Ordinary people were delighted for me. One man said 'The gardaí pursued the poor fellow and the State extradited him from America at huge cost and now they all have egg on their face.'

Carl thanked the jury for 'its considered verdict' and said I was very much obliged for all the help and assistance given to me during the trial. He said 'At long last Mr Gallagher has been vindicated.' And then he added the classic line: 'I hope his innocence is as widely publicised as his alleged guilt.'

Looking back on it all now, after seven years, I have mixed feelings. They were difficult times—I spent three years going bust—but I have a philosophical approach to it. I was very young and inexperienced. I didn't listen to the people I should have listened to and I made a couple of

*Not guilty—leaving the court with Richard Kean
after being acquitted*

mistakes that hit my career, my reputation and my ability to endorse or brand. The sad thing now is that although Peacock Alley was open for seven years, the only thing people will remember is the last year. They forget about the weddings, the birthday parties, the launches and the meals they raved about. Even now people come up to me and say 'I proposed to my wife after dinner in Peacock Alley', 'My son was conceived after New Year's Eve in Peacock Alley', 'The last really great meal I had before my husband died was in Peacock Alley.'

I often drive past the hotel, and I look back and think what a great opportunity it was for me. And I messed it all up. I admit that. I should have walked into it with my eyes open. I should have just done my restaurant, not the whole food operation. But by the time I realised that, I was too deep in the hole to trade out of it. I look at Kevin Thornton in there now—he probably got a softer landing than I did, because they definitely didn't want a second restaurant going broke on them. I imagine he got a much better deal than me because they could see that those numbers didn't work. It's as if they cut their teeth on me.

But the reality is—if it hadn't happened I wouldn't have met my wife, I wouldn't have had my two boys. Who knows what my life would have been.

In my view, the hotel had no idea this was going to snowball into the international, monumental mess-up for them it became. It was on Sky News and CNN and every time the Fitzwilliam Hotel was mentioned the painting thing came up. I imagine they were very sorry they ever started it. And I think that if they could turn back the clock they probably would.

I walked into the Shelbourne with my wife not long after I came back to Dublin to stay. Michael Holland and John Kavanagh and a few others were standing there. This was six years after the trial. I walked over to Michael with my hand out; he put his out and we shook hands.

The day I was acquitted my biggest problem was that I'd run out of money. I was living out of the back of the car and I knew I hadn't enough money to bring people to dinner that night. But my phone never stopped ringing and I sold a story to *Ireland on Sunday*. My legal team, my loyal friends and family—we all went off to Shanahans on the Green and had a lovely dinner. But I was shattered, battered and numb, it was no celebration for me , just the end of a nightmare. We finished the night when I sang

'The Green Fields of France' for Paul Mac and then we all headed off in different directions.

The lawyers had to be paid, of course. Over the next few months I earned good fees by going on various chat shows, writing a food column for the *Sunday World* and doing interviews with newspapers. In the autumn I went on the *Late Late Show*. It was my second time being interviewed by Pat Kenny on the show. (Gay Byrne had interviewed me when *New Irish Cooking* came out.) I was nervous about it, not knowing what sort of questions might be put, who might be in the audience with a grudge against me. But then I realised I had nothing to hide. If you're an entrepreneur you're a dreamer—you dream of it working, you don't dream of it not working—or you wouldn't do it. All I ever did was take a chance going into business, worked twenty hours a day, hired the right people, made a few bad decisions and ended up in the stew. And the interview was fine. Pat was very fair.

By the time I'd paid all my legal bills and everything else my funds were exhausted. I thought about suing for compensation but that would have meant more court cases. I wanted closure on the whole bloody thing, I didn't want to have any more to do with the paintings. But I did have to earn a living. I could see there was no future for me in Dublin. I was still an outcast. But where was I to go?

I'd gone for a break to South Africa, to Cape Town, soon after the trial and thought it was a great place—it's beautiful, it has a nice climate and property was cheap—I was thinking it was definitely a place I could live in. I stayed in the Table Bay Hotel,, which is part of the Sun

International Group. Some Irish people staying in the hotel recognised me and told the staff who I was and as it turned out, the chef had my cookbooks. Next thing, the director of operations for the group, Philip Georgas, introduced himself.

'Are you here on a holiday?'

'Yes, and I'm also having a little look around—I might consider moving here.'

'That's very interesting—will you come and speak to us if you do? We're looking for some help within our group with the food.'

Then five people started delivering breakfast in the morning—I was getting the royal treatment.

At that time I hadn't cooked professionally for over a year and I was beginning to miss the food business. I went back to Ireland and did the interview with the *Late Late Show*. I was still unsure about my future so I decided to go back to the States and look into opportunities there. I thought I'd probably end up as an executive chef in a hotel or something. I got offers from Las Vegas, San Francisco, New York and Washington and spent a week or two looking into them. But I was uncertain about the States, I really wanted to start off afresh. Meanwhile, Philip had contacted me a few times. He had told me that Sun International had about twenty resorts around Southern Africa and a number of high-class casinos and were looking for a food and beverage guru to come on board to shake them up and transform operations.

'Twenty resorts?' I said. 'That's an awful lot.'

'Well, you could possibly start with the Table Bay and upgrade that.' He said. 'We've done some research on you, we know the whole story about the paintings and that you went bust but we think you're the man to do it.' I'd said I'd think about it and get back to him.

By now I needed to make a living. So I called him and said I'd be prepared to go to South Africa for a year and I named my fee.

'I know it's going to be hugely challenging but if we do a deal I can be there in a week.'

He agreed immediately.

I said 'I'll get my attorney to draw up a contract and once it's signed I'll be on my way.' I sent the contract, they signed it, they paid the first month's fee into my account, I jumped on a plane and flew to South Africa.

And it was there that I met my beautiful wife.

Chapter 12
A place in the sun

ARRIVING IN CAPE TOWN, I knew I had a month or two to sharpen my teeth on the Table Bay Hotel. I also knew that since Sun International were paying me so much money as group executive chef and food and beverage consultant they wanted huge results. The CEO at the time was Peter Bacon, and he and Philip Georgas, director of operations, realised that the organisation needed drastic change and that it would take someone with my experience and background to do it.

I told them that before I did anything I would conduct an entire audit of the Table Bay Hotel from a standards point of view. So I looked at the banqueting, the room service, the breakfast, the pool food, the restaurants, the cleanliness of the kitchen, the operations within the kitchen, the quality of the produce, the productivity of the staff—everything.

The food and beverage manager brought me on a tour of the hotel—'Here's the storeroom, here's where we wash the glasses, here's where we make the coffee'. I'd sit in the restaurant and eat breakfast and watch everything. Then I'd go away and come back for lunch and dinner. I stayed in the hotel, of course, and I ordered room service. I looked at every single aspect of the hotel's food quality and service and then I wrote my report—it would make your hair stand on end, it was so detailed, and so critical.

Then I had to present my analysis to the board of directors, all of them sitting round a table, the managers, the CEO, the director of operations, and a couple of old grey-haired foxes.

I said 'My name is Conrad Gallagher. I've been hired as a consultant to the group and my first project is the Table Bay' and I went through all my findings and how I was going to fix the problems. There was a kind of a silence when I had finished. Then they asked a few questions and it became clear that they were quite concerned about my bullish approach, that I was going to upset people. But I said to them 'You know, it's really difficult to make an omelette without breaking eggs. But I'll tread as carefully as I can.'

Back into chef's whites in South Africa

Changing mindsets

Of course, once I started to make changes it ruffled a lot of feathers.

There was this whole leftover from apartheid. The management was entirely white, the workforce was not. The management was out of touch with what was going on with the employees, and they hated change. There was a lot of politics.

One thing that really amazed me was that the management had no hands-on role whatsoever. The head chef didn't cook, he just walked around with a clipboard or sent e-mails; the food and beverage manager sat in meetings all day.

There was a huge gap between them and the employees, a clear dividing line. I didn't like it, I felt that there was no cameraderie. I remember one of the managers saying to me soon after I started that the only time he ever rolled his sleeves up at work was when he had to point.

I said 'That's really awful—I'm a working guy. I woudn't be happy teaching somebody if I couldn't actually physically show them.'

There used to be this attitude at the Table Bay—'We're all ladies and gentlemen serving ladies and gentlemen'. I said to them, 'That's a load of rubbish—we're all employees serving paying customers so get that attitude out of your head right now. You're a staff member, paid a salary to do a job so you say "Good morning, Sir, good morning, Madam" and you get your guests whatever they want.'

I found that the employees were a really depressed

workforce because if they walked in and got a job as a butcher, they'd be doing that for thirty years. But I changed that. I said, 'If you're peeling onions today you'll be baking bread tomorrow, and I want you making soup next week and roasting chicken the week after.' I wanted them all to get a very rounded training. It was a huge effort because so many of them were simply not motivated. And that was down to bad management.

I had this thing called 'investing in the workforce'—it's something that is not done in South Africa. People would

I always like to teach by doing.

spend millions and millions of rand building hotels, and millions of rand on glasses and plates and if I asked them what their budget was to train staff they'd look at me as if I had ten heads. I used to say to them 'Forget about your fancy plates and your fancy silver cloches—give me thirty chefs for six months and a classroom and I'll train them'. They had very short-term thinking when it came to food and beverage staff. But I changed that and I got the right people to start listening to me.

I taught the chefs by way of master class with up to two hundred of them sitting in front of me. I would start off with tomatoes—slicing and deseeding, then I'd do onions and carrots, peeling and chopping, then I'd show them how to make coleslaw, slice beetroot, make salad dressings and make mayonnaise. Next it was how to roast chicken, roast lamb, roast duck, how to stuff produce, how to fillet fish and how to make basic sauces. Within time I started making it a basic condition that the head chefs in all the hotels in the group would give master classes to their staff.

Then there was the service Table Bay was offering its customers. I realised that I had a lot of work to do very quickly. The first thing I tackled was the breakfast because in a city hotel where guests like to go out for lunch and dinner it's the one meal that all the guests eat. I began with very basic things: instead of having orange juice and apple juice I had twenty different kinds of juice. Instead of buying in the juice I would freshly squeeze or liquidise different kinds of fruit and vegetable–grapefruit, spinach, carrot, blood orange, apple, cranberry; instead of regular eggs I'd do free range, ostrich eggs, hen's eggs.

This was a five star hotel but they couldn't get hot toast to the bedrooms in the morning. It was made in the kitchen and by the time the waiter was wheeling the trolley into the bedroom the toast would be cold. So I got the hotel to buy 100 toasters, one for each trolley, and the waiter would offer the guests a choice of six different types of bread and then he would toast it on the spot so it would be piping hot.

When the orange juice wasn't arriving up to the rooms with a nice froth still on top I got the hotel to buy juicers to put on the breakfast trolleys with a selection of fruit and the waiters would then prepare the fresh juice right there in the room.

Within a few days of transforming the breakfast, guests were going to reception and saying 'I had the most fantastic breakfast this morning—I've never had anything like it before.' Once the hotel saw what had happened with the breakfast they wanted the same for lunch, dinner and everything else. I was working eighteen hours a day.

After a couple of months the Table Bay was on the way to becoming a really interesting hotel with world-class standards. I pushed everybody—the managers, the employees, the purveyors, the suppliers. For example, previously the storeroom people were signing in food. I stopped that: it had to be the chef, sous chef or the food and beverage manager. How could the part-time bookkeeper downstairs sign in the food? From then on, somebody with an educated food-trained eye had to quality check it, it couldn't be done by an administrative person.

Next, instead of delivering twice a week they had to deliver seven days a week and produce had to be the freshest ever. I had to convince the suppliers to provide food that I would accept. I didn't want fruit and vegetables that had ever been near refrigeration, I wanted it from tree or soil right to the storeroom. It was the same high standards with the fish, the meat, the game. I turned the entire purchasing, hygiene and health and safety departments upsidedown and abolished their procedures.

Instead of the chefs coming in at seven in the morning they were coming in at four in the morning. Instead of the managers walking around in their suits, they had to put on an apron, do the mise en place, polish the cutlery, fix the lights, sort the music, make sure the staff's shoes were polished and their fingernails trimmed. I really embedded serious standards. Sun International soon wanted me to go on to the next hotel and the next hotel, to have them running on the same programme. The thing is, anyone can manage a hotel, anyone can build a hotel with 200 bedrooms and rooms for this and rooms for that, but very few can run a hotel with top food and beverage standards. Great food, a lively bar, good cocktails, the right atmosphere—they make the heartbeat of any good hotel. When you walk into the lobby, if you see a bustling bar, and busy restaurants and the locals are coming in you know you've come to the right place.

So over the next few years I rolled that out to other hotels in the group. I regularly flew up to Johannesburg to meet with Philip Georgas and his management team to discuss what I was going to be doing and what my plans were. I'd show them the menus and say 'we need a couple more staff here and a couple more there and I want to bring in a chef from Ireland'. I brought David Roche from the UK, Roger Moynihan from Northern Ireland and called up Mustapha Ouchbakou, my Moroccan pastry chef from Peacock Alley. We flew them in to Africa, and put them on one-year contracts.

I convinced Sun International to buy every single chef a pair of shoes, a chef's hat, chef's pants and a set of knives. I got them to clean up all the changing rooms and put in mirrors, and I used to say to the staff 'Look at yourself in the mirror and say "Look at me—I'm a chef. Look at me, I'm a waiter."' When they put on that uniform I wanted them to feel proud.

I got the kitchens cleaned and tidied up. If there were cracked tiles I got them replaced, if the lighting was dim I made them put in extra lighting. I got computers into rooms next to the kitchens so the chefs could go on the internet and download recipes. I got colour TVs into every single kitchen, and got them programmed on the Food Channel. I wanted the young people to see that if you were a good chef you could become a rock star, you could be on TV. It was something they could aspire to.

So by the time I had got the TVs in the kitchens, got the kitchens tidied up, changed all the menus, had every single chef in a uniform, and feeling proud, I had got a reputation for being a bit eccentric. I had a number of close shaves with human resources because I had a very no-nonsense approach to people, I preferred people who wanted to work. But I had the ear of the CEO and the director of operations.

I definitely upset a few people within Sun International because here I was rambling through the front doors of their hotels and telling them everything needed to be fixed, everything was wrong. In those days the executive chefs and the food and beverage managers used to sit behind their desks, drinking coffee and having meetings all day long. I forbade meetings during service hours, when breakfast, lunch and dinner were being served, I drove the managers on to the floors and pushed them to take active roles within the restaurants. I drove the executive chefs to their kitchens and made sure their offices were locked and their computers turned off –'Go fucking cook for the customers!' If I called a chef and he answered the phone in his office I would say 'Get to the fucking restaurant—your restaurant is full—what are you doing sitting in your office?'

I started getting so much attention that I was approached by the BBC—they had a very strong presence in Africa. They asked me could they do a film documentary where they would follow me around while I worked on transforming the remaining hotels in the group. So we did that over the next twelve months—in Zimbali Lodge, Wild Coast, Durban, in Zambia, Swaziland and up to Nigeria—I went all around the different hotels, driving standards, changing their breakfasts, their menus for lunch, high tea, dinner, transforming their big old dining rooms with no atmosphere, no service skills or enthusiasm into top class restaurants.

My wife

By that stage I had a good bit of money together, I'd bought a house. And I had met my wife to be.

It was a few months after I'd started working in Africa. I'd gone to Sun City, South Africa's answer to

Vegas, to the Palace Hotel, the next one on the list to be tackled. I was walking down the corridor with a group from Johannesburg and this beautiful five foot ten lady, with dark hair, gorgeous brown eyes and skin walked past. She kind of nodded her head and I nodded back and we all walked on. I turned round and asked one of the guys 'Who's that?' 'That's Candice Coetzee.'

Candice is from Port Elizabeth. She'd been a model and a beauty queen but when I met her she was doing all the PR and marketing for the gaming division. After a few days I convinced her to go on a date with me and it went on from there. Candice had to travel all round the resorts but no matter what happened we would always be back in Cape Town together on a Sunday. She would fly down and we would hang out together for the day. I really started enjoying the South African lifestyle—the beaches, the weather, the wineries. My relationship with Candice blossomed. She eventually moved in with me and we decided we'd have a life together. To our great delight, Candice fell pregnant and young Chandler was born on 18 May 2005.

My own thing again

Every Monday morning I'd be up early driving to the airport to go to Zambia, Nigeria, Swaziland, Namibia, Botswana. Around the time my contract with Sun International was coming up for renewal the BBC documentary—called *Conrad's Kitchen*—aired all over Africa, the Middle East, India and Egypt. Other hotel groups started contacting me with offers and other opportunities were coming in. Sun International were keen for me to stay on. I said I would stay as their food and beverage consultant but I would move out of their head office and open up on my own under the name Conrad Gallagher Consulting. I would be more of an independent agent, a contractor working for them. I also took on other clients—I wanted to expand into Dubai and the Middle East. I agreed that I would spend the first fifteen days of the month with Sun International, and the rest of the month I would work with my other clients in Pakistan or Egypt or wherever.

Once a month I was on a private plane so I could go round all the hotels within two or three days. Every head chef that worked with me had to sit down every month with every single one of his employees, from the cleaner to the lettuce washer to the butcher to the guy baking the bread, and give them a set of objectives. At the end of the month he had to do an appraisal of how each one had done. The head chef then had to sit down with me for half a day and go through every single person that worked for him and report on their progress. With that system I knew every chef would be trained, he would be told what his weak points were, what his strong points were.

What I was doing was grooming the young staff to take over from the big, rich fatties called chefs and managers sitting in their offices. I knew that if I had paper trails for the young chefs from the time they started with us as kids that within five years they would be the sous chefs and the head chefs—that was my ambition, that was my mission statement to the company.

I stayed with Sun International for six years in total, from 2003 to 2009. I spent those years trying to change people's mindsets—not just the managers' but also the workers' mentality. I would say to them 'It's not about walking into work doing as little as you can and then leaving'. I always taught them that they would get back what they put in. I tried to teach them that if they came to work with enthusiasm and excitement and a will to do better they would personally do better—and get satisfaction from every minute.

During the first few years I made good contacts and a lot of money. I bought the house and a few apartments. Candice left Sun International to come and work with me. I'd hired a PA, two full time concept designers, and a culinary PA for everything to do with the food and the restaurants. I'd been working with Starwoods and St Regis, I had two new clients in Saudi Arabia and a family of clients in Pakistan.

I started building restaurant concepts for other top hotels around the world, offering them a turnkey package. If they were building a hotel with, say, 200 bedrooms and they knew they had to have four restaurants I would fly into that area, do a quick study of the other hotels and see what the other restaurants were doing. I'd come back a week later and say 'OK, I think you should do a really nice Moroccan restaurant, a New York style steak house, an Asian fusion style rest and an Italian trattoria.' They'd agree and I would then go away and myself and my staff would fill a 90-page document with my interpretation of an Italian trattoria, and within that would be mood boards, menus, crockery type, tabletop settings, everything from the type of lights to tables, chairs, floor finishes, special features, the kind of staff needed to run it. I would sell each one of those concepts for anything between $20,000 and $30,000.

At any one time during that period I had a number of projects going. I'd bring the concept to reality, train staff, spend three or four weeks there before the opening,and another few weeks after the opening and on some occasions I'd be back visiting every month for a couple of days until everything was running smoothly.

While I was travelling up and down to Sun International and up and down to Dubai, to Pakistan, to Abu Dhabi, Candice would be in the office running the entire network of interior designers, architects, kitchen designers and everything else. We started getting a really lucrative business going.

We rented out the first house and when Chandler was six months old we bought an eight-bedroom mansion in the centre of the winelands of Constantia. Life was really, really good. The year after we moved into the house we got married—on 15 December 2005. The wedding was in our house, on our own grounds, with 150 friends and family—it was a special time.

And then the wheel turned.

Chapter 13
The wheel turns

ONE MORNING IN LATE SUMMER 2006 I woke up in pain. And I knew straight away that it was the same pain as the one that I'd had in Baggot Street all those years ago. I said to Candice 'It's back again.' It was familiar, I knew what it was. For about six months I'd felt that something was wrong. I called my oncologist and asked him to organise an ultrasound for that day.

'I'm not feeling good, I've got that lump again, there's definitely something wrong with me.'

He didn't take me seriously at first.

'Conrad, you're always fussing, don't worry about this, it's something simple.'

'Can you arrange an ultrasound or not?'

'Yes, I can.'

He booked me in for 11.30 a.m. As I left for the hospital, I said to Candice, 'Don't expect me back today. I can tell this is serious.'

While I was having the ultrasound I said to the guy doing it, 'There's a tumour there, isn't there?' He said to me, 'Mr Gallagher, you seem like a fairly straightforward man. Normally the procedure is that I tell your oncologist and he tells you but . . . yes, I see something.'

It was another tumour on my remaining testicle. I knew the score. After talking to the oncologist I went out to the waiting room and called Candice.

'Bad news, darling, it's another tumour. They want to operate again.'

I was on the operating table next morning and my second testicle was removed. It had to be done to save my life. It is very rare for someone to get cancer in both testicles so my medical team needed to get advice on what to do after the surgery. They consulted different doctors in America and professors from around the world to see what was the best course to follow. A major problem was that with the second testicle removed my system had no way of creating testosterone—without it my body couldn't function.

The doctors went through all the different options with me and what I was facing. It was decided that I would have a series of bouts of chemotherapy—there would be no radiation this time. They warned me that the chemo would be quite intense—combined with the lack of natural testosterone, it would knock me for a number of months.

'You will never be able to have children again,' they told me. That really upset me. 'You will have to have artificial testosterone injected once a month for the rest of your life and your body will never be the same again because artificial testosterone is very different from the natural sort.' From now on if I was to be sexually active it would almost have to be done chemically. And slowly but surely my limbs would get stiffer.

Now I had to prepare for my life to be very different.

I cleared my schedule, told Sun International I was going to be out of action for three months, and started the chemo. It was very, very severe. There was no working through it this time, it wasn't like Baggot Street. It really knocked me out. It practically killed me. This was chemo, then bed, chemo, bed. There was nothing else.

A little miracle happened around then. I started the chemo and began to try to come to terms with the fact that I would have no more children. Next thing, Candice called me and said 'Guess what? I'm pregnant!' She had conceived seven days before my operation. Conor was born the following year, on 20 March 2007.

Candice suffered really badly from morning sickness. She had a tough pregnancy from the beginning. And obviously because it was our last chance she didn't want to push herself. For a number of months we were both very sick. It took me two or three months to recover from the chemo. There are still continuing after effects—as well as my limbs stiffening, I get hot and cold flushes, especially around the time of the injections, and all the chemo I've had has resulted in me getting out of breath very easily. And then there were the psychological effects. I agreed to have implants for cosmetic reasons so at least I would look right.

The year passed. Now, we just wanted to get to Christmas, have a break and try to decide about our future. One of the hardest things that started getting into my head was the worry about how my family would fare if anything happened to me—how would Candice keep going, what would happen to the kids? I asked myself was the return of the cancer telling me something, was it a sign that I should start slowing down?

We went back about our lives. Any time you get an illness you start eating better and you start going to Mass more, you start exercising or going to the gym, you really promise yourself that you'll become healthier and look after yourself. But then you slowly start going back to your old ways, eating late at night, not exercising as much as you should, you start being naughty again.

Writing on the wall

I'd never felt totally content in South Africa. There had been times when I'd thought 'Yes, this is a good place, I'll probably stay here forever' but more often I'd wake up in the morning thinking 'this place is not real, it's too artificial.' We'd drive out on the road in the morning and see all these people living in awful poverty, in shacks, and then there'd be us in our big car off to our eight-bedroomed house in the winelands. I know I was guilty of the lifestyle and I loved it. But there was also a side of me that said 'I'm Irish, I definitely don't want my children brought up in this kind of society. I want my children to grow up in Ireland'. I was also missing Lauren more and more.

All the time we were in South Africa we used to go back to Ireland three or four times a year and see Lauren as much as possible, and she used to come out to Cape Town and my parents used to visit. But I had felt for a long time that we should all be closer, so that Lauren and her brothers could be together more.

Then there was the security aspect. There were stories every day about break-ins and kidnaps and women being raped and kids being murdered—we were always terrified of that happening. We had a very high tech security system, cameras in all the rooms, 18-foot high walls around the house with electric wires on top, sensors all over the gardens and panic buttons to press if there was a problem. But it wasn't enough.

One morning when I was due to fly to Durban I got up at a quarter to five and went downstairs. There was a guest apartment attached to the house, and we were sleeping there at the time because the main house was being decorated. It was connected to the house through the garage, and as soon as I opened the door to the kitchen I heard voices. Each room had a little camera to see if there was any activity and I could see on the monitor that there were strangers in our house, about 12 of them all carrying guns—it was a break-in.

I turned around, closed the door and went back upstairs again. I was terrified for the kids and for Candice. There had been break-ins in the area but this was the first time ever that I felt our lives were threatened. I managed to get upstairs, secure Candice and the kids and press the panic button. Within a few minutes five police cars and security trucks had arrived.

The robbers had cleared out the house—they took everything, even Chandler's toys, and they left dirty fingerprints all over his bedroom. After that Candice would never stay in the house on her own again. We'd spent thirteen months renovating it, it was the home of our dreams, the most fantastic house you could ever imagine, but we couldn't live in it any more.

By this time I'd started travelling again, about twenty days a month. So we put the house on the market a week or two after the break in, and moved back into town, back to our first house on Ocean View Drive, and started having a bit of a town life again. That's where we lived for the rest of our time in South Africa.

I had said to Candice that I would start cutting back on my travelling. But when I got the cancer I'd had to stall a lot of the commitments I'd taken on so when I did go back to work I was flat out for the next eighteen months.

I organised Oprah Winfrey's New Year's Eve party for 150 guests in The Palace Hotel, Sun City. I always used to enjoy devising and presenting special events—like dinner at midnight on a beach by the Indian Ocean, with the food cooked over fires, or transforming the Zimbali Lodge outdoor dining room into a Bollywood-style Versailles—chandeliers wrapped in orange chiffon, ostrich plumes, musicians playing sitars, dancers, hundreds of candles. The menu for that event was baked local oysters with a coconut and curry foam, Scottish salmon cured with tea and lime leaves, garnished with caviar in cucumber oil, quail stuffed with capers, truffles and foie gras, sorbet of passion fruit with fromage blanc.

But of course every event meant being away from home for days if not weeks. By this time Conor was nearly two and Chandler was four. And when I went away it really started affecting them. If I went to Saudi Arabia for a week or ten days or if I went to Dubai, by the time I got back the kids started to become distant. I had to keep rebuilding my relationship with them—they kept pushing me away when I travelled.

One day Candice sat me down and said, 'Conrad, I got married to share my life with somebody—the kids and I are spending twenty days a month alone. You're making great money, but we never see you any more and anytime you are home you're always too tired. Can we stop right here?'

So I agreed that from that point on I wouldn't take on any new clients. I reduced my commitment with Sun International to just a couple of their hotels and told them that instead of doing twenty days a month I'd only be doing ten. Myself and Candice spent the next couple of months getting our lives back on track, spending time with the kids.

When I stopped travelling I missed being hands-on in food, so we opened a restaurant called Geisha, serving Thai food, in a great location in the hub of Cape Town just across from the Stadium where the World Cup was to take place in 2010. We also had a couple of coffee shops.

Geisha did really well but six months after opening we were forced to relocate. The owners of the building wanted to knock it down and build a hotel in time for the World Cup, which they never actually did. We'd invested heavily in the restaurant and having to move it obviously cost us a lot.

In December 2008 I was again in charge of the food operations for the Nedbank Golf Challenge, doing 20,000 meals a day for about nine days. Every year I would try to make it better than the year before—better food, better profits, every year by the time I'd finished I'd be planning the next one. I do big numbers really well and I pride myself on being able to give restaurant quality food to thousands of people. I had a reputation around the world—if you're doing a function for 20,000 people Conrad Gallagher is the guy you should be talking to. But that year I dropped about 20 lbs over the nine days and by the end of it I was physically and mentally exhausted.

When that was over, and I was home again I could see Candice's demeanour changing. Every day I would go down to the restaurant and the coffee shops and Candice could see that by the 15th of January I'd be back at work and it would be the same story—just seeing each other at the weekend. I had also realised that it was impossible for me to make a living just in Cape Town. Its season lasts only four or five months—the rest of the time it's like a ghost town.

We agreed then that when the kids finished school in June we would move back to Ireland, and that I would commute back and forth until my contract finished in September.

I didn't know that from January to June 2009 would be my six toughest months in business.

Crash

I had got involved in the property business, both personally and with two property professionals—I was joint and several with them. Like so many others I lost everything. The signs had been there for a while, it was becoming harder to sell, and harder to rent but then the government brought in a Credit Act which drastically restricted credit, and interest rates went up to 16 per cent. People in the middle of developments couldn't finish them and practically overnight the demand for property collapsed—so many people were over-borrowed, including ourselves. And of course we'd bought at the top of the market—everyone was so optimistic, 'The World

Cup's coming, the only way is up . . .' We were left with properties that we couldn't rent and we couldn't sell but we had the mortgages to pay. The collapse was really sudden. It was like somebody creeping up behind you with a mallet and hitting you over the back of the head.

In South Africa if you're late for a month with your mortgage payment the bank writes you a letter; if you're late for two months they write you a letter of demand and if you haven't paid within 90 days they start the repossession process. Then the cleaver and the axe are right down on top of you. An attorney, a trustee, is appointed over your entire assets—unlike in Ireland or the UK—and you lose control overnight. That's exactly what happened to me. You wake up one morning and somebody else controls your money. All your bank accounts are frozen, your credit cards are frozen, you're told they're going to take every single thing you have. I was made bankrupt.

It was almost as if my world came to an end again. There were media reports all over the world, the same type of headlines as before. I was called every horrible name under the sun. It was horrendous. I remember driving in Cape Town one day during the summer—Candice and the kids were at home in Ireland by this time—and I suddenly started to shake all over. I had to pull in, I thought I was having a heart attack, that I was going to die. And all the time I was saying to myself, 'What have I done? How can this be happening again?'

I had my wife and children to think about. Candice was in a country that she'd visited but had never lived in—I had to keep the show going. I was back and forth to Ireland and in the autumn I moved back permanently.

I had to keep reassuring my wife that everything would be all right but she was strong and stood by me.

My exit from South Africa was not the way I planned it, but the control was taken out of my hands, all I could do was pick up the pieces and keep moving. I had to rise above all the scathing media coverage and keep going for the sake of my family.

About three months after I was bankrupted and was settled back in Ireland, I was driving home one day. I went into Donnybrook Fair and got coffee and a couple of other things. Walking past the news stand I saw my name in headlines in three newspapers so I bought them as well. I drove around to Herbert Park, parked and started to read. It was the first time I'd looked at a paper since my return.

All of a sudden I could feel the blood rushing from my head to my toes. A cold sweat came over me. What would these headlines, this name calling, do to my kids, what would it do to my wife? I'd tried to build up security for my family, bought houses, apartments—and I'd managed to lose everything—again. I sat there in my car in Herbert Park and I cried for an hour. There wasn't a tear left inside me by the time I stopped. And between that happening and arriving home I'd told myself that I needed to be strong. I wasn't allowed to let people get inside my head. I said to myself 'They don't know the truth, they don't know that I have worked sixteen, eighteen hours a day every day of my life, they don't understand the efforts I've made to try to invest in a workforce, the efforts I've made to train people, they don't realise the sacrifices I've made, working twenty days a month away from my family to try and build a secure future.'

I decided that from that day on I'd be as strong as an ox for my kids and my wife, I'd build a shield around myself from then on. The mistakes I've made in the past would keep coming back at me but I'd pick myself up, again.

Chapter 14
Lessons learned

AFTER WE'D BEEN BACK in Ireland for a while, I decided to set up my own place. Not for the first time people thought I was mad. 'Opening restaurants in a recession? Is that wise?' they said. But I knew that I could learn from my experiences and do something that stood a chance. And it's working so far. Both Salon des Saveurs in Dublin and Conrad's Kitchen in Sligo are doing really well and we now employ nearly fifty people. We recently ran a promotion that was so popular it crashed the website.

The difference this time is that now I realise I'm an entrepreneur. I've been working with food and in restaurants for over twenty-five years, but it's only over the last year or so that it kind of dawned on me that there's a big difference between being a chef and being a restaurateur. Being a chef is all about ambition and making a name; the food is all about *you*, what you think and what you want and indulging your creativity. I used to pour so much energy into working twelve services a week that I took my eye off the other stuff, the numbers. I put the food, and quality and standards before profits, and of course no business can survive if it's not making a profit.

Now I know I have to offer the customers something I want to sell and they want to buy. For Salon for example,

I decided on a delicious tasting menu with a set price per head so people know exactly what the meal is going to cost them. These days customers do their research before they come out, they don't want any surprises. The menu is very seasonal—in winter lots of root vegetables and warming slow-cooked dishes; in spring morels come in and asparagus (one of my suppliers' specialities) then lovely baby beetroots, Irish strawberries, fresh lobsters, and then the salmon and trout season starts. I like to support small producers, and I buy organic whenever I can. The focus is always on taste and flavour. We also do all my staples that were so popular over the years —seared scallops with foie gras, risotto with butternut squash, pastrami salmon and ravioli of spiced crab with butternut squash. People come in and are delighted when they see something they recognise: 'Oh, the last time we had daube of beef was in Peacock Alley'.

We also gave the restaurant a familiar, comfortable feeling, almost retro, so that when you go in you feel that you've been there before. I don't think cutting-edge modern is what the market wants at the moment—people want comfort and warmth.

This time round I'm really on top of the business side as well. I get very good advice on what I'm doing and I have a very good financial team, but I talk to my head chefs and managers every day and make sure they are very aware on a daily basis of how the business is doing, so if I call them up and ask are we up or down, I get an instant answer. We do stock takes every morning and I know every day's sales figures. I keep two live spreadsheets on my computer where I input turnover and cost of sales so every day I know the ratio of purchases to sales and can find out how we're doing compared to the previous week.

There's a little side of me still that will go for standards over profits but I know every bill that has to be paid and I cost every recipe. Staff can only order up to a certain limit and beyond that I have to approve it. If the electricity bill jumps 100 euros one month I'll want to know why; if a bottle of wine goes missing I'll know about it two days later. I work off a budget and if we're missing targets I make adjustments as necessary by changing staff rosters, schedules and menus. Everything is done methodically—it's very well balanced, well thought out and calculated.

It took three or four months to get everything running smoothly and stabilise the team, but I was persistent as I always am, so I just kept going till I got it right. Suppliers were another thing. No-one wanted to give credit, so I pay cash. It suits both sides as it happens because they need the instant cash flow and it keeps my books straight. In the beginning I wasn't able to accept credit cards because we didn't have an ADSL line so it was just cash or cheques. But that worked really well for us, and we decided to continue that way—it saves all the charges.

Conrad's Kitchen, Sligo

Then there's Conrad's Kitchen in Sligo. After about six months of trading well I was ready to look for another opening. Salon is a small restaurant, with only 55 covers, so with a young family I really needed to expand a bit. I was invited to set up a restaurant in the Model Arts Gallery in Sligo. The idea really appealed to me so I started looking for a head chef for Salon, so that I could be sure that the standards would be kept up even when I don't spend all day in Dublin. None of the people we tried worked out, so when Matthew Fuller, my sous chef, who had worked with me in Peacock Alley, asked for a chance, we jumped at it. He's one of the finest cooks I've ever worked with , and I look forward to seeing him grow.

Ten years ago if I'd been setting up a restaurant in Sligo I would have said to myself: 'Ah, sure, they'll drive from all over the country to eat my food'. I would have gone in and given the Sligo people what I thought they should have and tried to shake up the whole food scene.

Now it's different. It's not about that any more. This time round it's about being a rock, and creating something solid and true that will last. Sligo is a small cosmopolitan town in a good catchment area, close to Donegal and Enniskillen, and has a seasonal tourist trade. But I have to ask myself how day-to-day business will flow, what it will be like on a wet Tuesday in winter, who will come in during January.

The answer is it's local, it has to be a local restaurant for a local audience. So I take old-style food, the classics—crab cakes, prawn cocktail, Caesar salads, risottos, T-bone ribeye steak and lambshank shepherd's pie—and do them to the highest quality possible. The prawn cocktail is made with beautiful fresh prawns, cooked in their shells in court bouillon to retain all the juice and sweetness, then quickly cooled on crushed ice and refrigerated for six hours. They're then peeled and served with carpaccio of beetroot, really good avocado, homemade mayonnaise and Marie Rose sauce.

Then there's the lambshank shepherd's pie. We marinade the lambshank for 48 hours, then slow cook it for 12 hours, and allow it to cool in its cooking liquor. Then the liquor is strained and reduced by half and the meat is shredded and folded into the sauce along with sautéed brunois of shallots, leeks, celery, carrot, and butternut squash. I serve it with lovely little baby vegetables and basil mashed potato.

The key to the quality is the produce. Take the T-bone steak. I never would have done that before, it would have seemed too simple. I would have done complicated dishes and put huge effort into the garnish and the presentation. Now, I focus on the actual meat. I know the farmer who rears the beef. I've visited his farm, I've seen the way he grazes the cattle and how he feeds them—I've even tasted the nuts he gives them. I went into the whole process. He has his own abattoir and we agreed that he hangs the beef for 45 days in a controlled temperature and he cuts it exactly the way I want. Then we hang it for another couple of days before serving it. So it's not just a rib-eye on a plate, it's a top class piece of beef and I serve it with great Béarnaise sauce and handcut chips cooked in duck fat.

(It wasn't always like this. In 1995, when I came back to Ireland from Monte Carlo and put daube of beef on the menu in Morel's, I asked the butchers for ox cheeks. They looked at me as if I'd grown horns—they didn't want to split the heads and pull out the cheeks. And it was the same with lambshanks—I'd call up and say 'I want five lambshanks' and the butcher would say 'What the hell am I going to do with the rest of the leg?')

CONRAD GALLAGHER

The main elements

Running the restaurants is no longer just about me being in the kitchen, it has to work as a business. It's not just about the food or hype—there's no longevity in that. It's about the whole package: customers, employees and suppliers. I now spend my time building and managing relationships with customers and suppliers, treating employees right, stock taking, purchasing properly, being responsible and balancing my time evenly. It's taken me many years to realise the importance of all these things.

It starts with the customers. They have to be happy. It's about opening the door and welcoming them to make them sure they know they are appreciated and that I want them to come back. If one of my regular customers is celebrating something in my restaurant—a birthday, or an anniversary, even if it's my day off, or I've been called away, I try to be there for at least some of the time. I know they'll be disappointed if I don't come out and greet them—it's important to them and it's important to me. And of course they have to know you're out there so marketing is hugely important and I spend a lot of time on it.

Then there are the employees—if you don't take care of them you'll lose them, you can't work them to the bone, they have to be paid properly and they have to be empowered to play a certain role and feel part of the successes—and the failures.

Sometimes I might need to step in and manage relationships with my suppliers. My sous chef might have fought for three or four days with the fish supplier over quality issues, for example. Egos may get involved and they tell each other to fuck off and then there's a stalemate and I have to come in and sit down and say to my chef, 'You shouldn't have told him to fuck off and hit him with a lobster on the back of his head'. Then I'll respectfully point out to the fish supplier that he shouldn't have brought the lobster if it wasn't moving.

A typical day

I get up around 6.30, and watch the news on the TV. Then I'll grind some coffee beans—selecting and blending them is a hobby I really enjoy—and make a double espresso. I get the boys their milk—one of them likes it hot, one likes it cold. I like to have it ready for them as soon as they're awake. My wife will be up and about by that stage. I make the kids' sandwiches and then we all go off on the school run. It takes about half an hour and it's a great catching up time because by the time I get home at night everybody is asleep.

We drop the kids at school and then I go in to one of my restaurants. I alternate between the two, so one day I'll do lunch in Dublin and dinner in Sligo, and the next day I'll do lunch in Sligo and dinner in Dublin. It can be a bit of an endurance test at times, I might be tired after the late night and the drive, but as soon as I arrive at the restaurant the adrenalin kicks in.

Things will be buzzing already in the kitchen—the stocks and sauces will be on, the bread will be proving; in the dining room they'll be ironing the tablecloths and arranging the flowers. I'll be looking at all the things that need to be done and at the things that aren't quite right. There are so many things to watch out for that I'm usually firing off a dozen questions. 'How's the bread? The Guinness bread should be a wee bit darker. How's the crust on the tomato bread? Let me see the prawns. Let me taste the Caesar dressing. Is that the wine sauce?—I think it needs a bit more reducing. Is the sauce shiny enough? Has that beef been aged long enough?' (If it goes out with two or three days less ageing than I want it'll annoy me—the customers mightn't always spot it but I'll know and it'll upset me.)

And at the same time my book-keeeper might ring about the wine direct debit or something. Before I would have said 'Don't annoy me with that, I'm busy cooking,' now I say 'OK. I'll transfer some money.' And I'll be asking 'Is the newsletter ready to go out? Have we answered all the e-mails this morning?'

I cook from half twelve to half two, but I'm no longer in first thing in the morning peeling the onions, and I'm no longer the last to leave. I used to feel that nobody could make things better than me. But now I train the team to do the sauces, the bread, the desserts and the ice creams—I'm a natural teacher.

At the end of service if I've pushed myself as hard as I can, driven myself and the team and we have happy customers in the restaurant, we'll all be happy and I'll finish on a natural high. But if I haven't done my utmost best, if I've let something go, I'll be disappointed with myself. Maybe it's the Catholic guilt thing, it'll hang over me.

It's important of course to leave some energy in the tank at the end of the week to give my family what they need from me. Now that I'm very much a family man my philosophy and attitude have changed. Sometimes people get riled up in one of my restaurants and it reminds me of how I was twenty years ago. If someone annoyed me back then I would have thought 'this guy's an asshole—I don't want to talk to him' and I'd have thrown him out. Now I let my experience get me through it. I let him finish, then calmly and politely suggest his approach could be better and that we could talk it through.

Lessons learned

My life has been a rollercoaster. I went from a small town in Ireland cooking turkey and ham to cooking for the President in the White House and holding a Michelin star during my years in Peacock Alley. I've also suffered three of the worst things that could happen to a person— bankruptcy, cancer and prison. But I've come back each time. Hopefully, I can sail through my forties and fifties and build security for my family and there'll be no more turbulence.

Things are different now. I don't socialise much. I love to spend time with Candice, and I look forward to quiet mornings on the river bank in Straffan Co. Kildare. When I look at my three treasures I think if that is how wealth is measured then I'm a very wealthy man.

Index

INDEX

INDEX

INDEX

INDEX

14·99